How To Use This Study Guide

This 10-lesson study guide corresponds to *"Christ's Message to Thyatira"* *With Rick Renner* (Renner TV). Each lesson in this study guide covers a topic that is addressed during the program series, with questions and references supplied to draw you deeper into your own private study of the Scriptures on this subject.

To derive the most benefit from this study guide, consider the following:

First, watch or listen to the program prior to working through the corresponding lesson in this guide. (Programs can also be viewed at **renner.org** by clicking on the Media/Archives links or on our Renner Ministries YouTube channel.)

Second, take the time to look up the scriptures included in each lesson. Prayerfully consider their application to your own life.

Third, use a journal or notebook to make note of your answers to each lesson's Study Questions and Practical Application challenges.

Fourth, invest specific time in prayer and in the Word of God to consult with the Holy Spirit. Write down the scriptures or insights He reveals to you.

Finally, take action! Whatever the Lord tells you to do according to His Word, do it.

For added insights on this subject, it is recommended that you obtain Rick Renner's book *Signs You'll See Just Before Jesus Comes*. You may also select from Rick's other available resources by placing your order at **renner.org** or by calling 1-800-742-5593.

TOPIC

The History of Thyatira

SCRIPTURES

1. **Revelation 2:18** — And unto the angel of the church in Thyatira write....

GREEK WORD

1. "angel" — ἄγγελος (*angelos*): a human messenger or angel; one sent on a special mission; one dispatched to perform a specific assignment; a delegate or dignitary; pictures the role of a pastor; a messenger of God

2. "church" — ἐκκλησία (*ekklesia*): a called, separated assembly; a prestigious assembly of distinguished citizens who determined laws, debated public policy, formulated new policies, argued and ruled in judicial matters, elected chief magistrates, and decided who should be banished; a body of believers who have been called out, called forth, selected, and assembled to be God's representatives in every town, city, state, or nation; a body called to make decisions that affect the atmosphere of a region

SYNOPSIS

The ten lessons in this study on **Christ's Message to Thyatira** will focus on the following topics:

- The History of Thyatira
- Intelligence and Judgment
- A Church Committed to Good Works
- What Jesus Thinks About Compromise in the Church
- Ahab and Jezebel
- What Does "Space To Repent" Mean?
- What Is Repentance?
- What Causes God To Judge Someone Today?

A Note From Rick Renner

I am on a personal quest to see a "revival of the Bible" so people can establish their lives on a firm foundation that will stand strong and endure the test as the end-time storm winds begin to intensify.

In order to experience a revival of the Bible in your personal life, it is important to take time each day to read, receive, and apply its truths to your life. James tells us that if we will continue in the perfect law of liberty — refusing to be forgetful hearers but determined to be doers — we will be blessed in our ways. As you watch or listen to the programs in this series and work through this corresponding study guide, I trust that you will search the Scriptures and allow the Holy Spirit to help you hear something new from God's Word that applies specifically to your life. I encourage you to be a doer of the Word that He reveals to you. Whatever the cost, I assure you — it will be worth it.

> Thy words were found, and I did eat them;
> and thy word was unto me the joy and rejoicing of mine heart:
> for I am called by thy name, O Lord God of hosts.
> — Jeremiah 15:16

Your brother and friend in Jesus Christ,

Rick Renner

Christ's Message to Thyatira

Copyright © 2019 by Rick Renner
1814 W. Tacoma St.
Broken Arrow, OK 74012-1406

Published by Rick Renner Ministries
www.renner.org

ISBN 13: 978-1-6803-1620-9

ISBN 13 eBook: 978-1-6803-1658-2

- The Depths of Satan Inside the Church
- Hold Fast and Occupy Until Jesus Comes

The emphasis of this lesson:

The city of Thyatira has been around for thousands of years. In early New Testament times, it was rebuilt to be a barrier of defense for the city of Pergamum. Along with a strong military presence, there was also a strong church — a church that Christ spoke to in Revelation 2.

The city of Thyatira was located about 40 kilometers (or about 25 miles) east of the city of Pergamum. To understand Thyatira, one must understand Pergamum and its importance. Pergamum was the seat of the proconsul for the entire province of Asia. Thus, it was home to many politicians and wealthy people — a royal city filled with great treasure and marked by magnificence. As such, it was the target of invaders from the east who wanted to attack and plunder it. Thyatira was built to be a blockade to stop eastern invaders. Not only was there a strong military presence there, but there was also a strong presence of God. During the First Century, a church was established in the city — one of the seven churches Jesus spoke to in Revelation 2. His words to the believers in Thyatira are still applicable to us today. Thus, we need to know and understand what He said.

John Had Been Imprisoned on the Isle of Patmos

The book of Revelation is Jesus' revelation of Himself to the apostle John and to us. During the reign of Emperor Domitian, John was exiled to the isle of Patmos as a political prisoner. Patmos was a forbidden island out in the middle of the sea, stripped of all its vegetation. When John and his associate were deposited on the island, they were left with the arduous task of foraging for food and securing water each day. For living quarters, they secured a desolate cave positioned atop a mountain. It was in that cave that the risen Christ appeared to John and gave him what we know today as the book of Revelation.

In Revelation 1:10, John said, "I was in the Spirit on the Lord's day, and heard behind me a great voice, as of a trumpet." The words "I was" in Greek is the word *ginomai*, which describes *something completely unexpected; something that takes one off guard or by surprise.* The use of the word *ginomai* informs us that what John experienced that day was totally unanticipated.

John said, "I was in the Spirit...." The word "spirit" in the *King James Version* is capitalized, but in the Greek, it is lowercased. Thus, the phrase "in the spirit" indicates *in the spirit realm* or *in the dimension of the spirit*. John was saying, "I came to find myself lifted out of the physical realm and placed into the dimension of the spirit." It was in the spirit realm that John heard the voice of Jesus.

Jesus Spoke to Seven Specific Churches

In Revelation 1:12, John went on to say, "And I turned to see the voice that spake with me. And being turned, I saw seven golden candlesticks." We know from Scripture that the seven golden candlesticks are representative of the seven largest and most influential churches that were located in the province of Asia. For two entire chapters — Revelation 2 and 3 — Jesus spoke a very specific message to each of these seven churches.

He began with the church of Ephesus and then moved to the church of Smyrna, the church of Pergamum, the church of Thyatira, the church of Sardis, the church of Philadelphia, and, finally, the church of Laodicea. These cities were not just a random selection. They were all located in sequence on a road and connected with each other. By addressing these seven particular churches, Jesus addressed all the problems in the entire Church that existed at that time. In fact, the issues He addressed then are the same issues the Church has been facing for the last 2,000 years.

Right in the middle of the seven churches was *the church of Thyatira*, and in Revelation 2:18-21, Jesus spoke these words:

> And unto the angel of the church in Thyatira write; These things saith the Son of God, who hath his eyes like unto a flame of fire, and his feet are like fine brass; I know thy works, and charity, and service, and faith, and thy patience, and thy works; and the last to be more than first.
>
> Notwithstanding I have a few things against thee, because thou sufferest that woman Jezebel, which calleth herself a prophetess, to teach and to seduce my servants to commit fornication, and to eat things sacrificed unto idols. And I gave her space to repent of her fornication; and she repented not.

Pastors Are God's Appointed 'Angels' in the Church

First, notice the word "angel" in verse 18: "Unto the angel of the church in Thyatira write…." The word "angel" is the Greek word *angelos*, which describes *a human messenger or angel; one sent on a special mission; one dispatched to perform a specific assignment;* or *a delegate or dignitary.* Although the word *angelos* can describe a heavenly being, in this passage it pictures *the role of a pastor* or *a messenger of God.*

To be clear, angels from Heaven don't preach or teach the Word of God. It is not their job to bring correction to a church. That is the calling of humans in whom God has entrusted the fivefold ministry gifts (*see* Ephesians 4:11,12). Pastors are shepherds of Christ's Church, and when He wants to speak a word of commendation or a word of correction to a congregation, He speaks it first and foremost to the pastor.

Jesus honors and does not bypass the spiritual authority He established. The pastor is the head of the local church, and he is the first one to hear what Christ has to say. His job is to listen and assimilate what the Lord is saying, incorporating it into his own life first. Then, to the best of his ability, he is to clearly communicate the message to the people of the church.

In many ways, your pastor is like an angel to you. He is God's anointed and appointed dignitary sent to preach and teach the Word, helping you grow and mature into the likeness of Jesus. Take time to pray for your pastor and his family. Ask the Lord to clothe him in humility so that he can clearly hear what the Spirit is saying to him and your church.

What Is 'the Church'?

Next, notice that Christ's message was directed to the angel of "the church." The word "church" here is not the physical buildings where people meet. On the contrary, it refers to *the people.*

The word "church" is the Greek word *ekklesia*, which is a compound of the word *ek*, meaning *out*, and the word *klesia*, a form of the word *kaleo*, which means *to call.* When these words are joined to form the word *ekklesia*, it describes *a called, separated assembly that has been called out from the world for a specific purpose.*

New Testament writers fully understood the meaning of the word *ekklesia*. It was a very familiar term borrowed from the pagan world, originating from the city of Athens. The word *ekklesia* described a group of citizens that met regularly on a hill near the Parthenon. These individuals were called out from the Athenian society to determine laws, debate public policy, formulate new policies, argue and rule in judicial matters, and elect chief magistrates. To be a part of this distinguished group was very prestigious. They had the power to change the atmosphere of their communities.

What was true of the Church then is still true today. Since its birth, the Church of the Lord Jesus Christ — the *ekklesia* — has consisted of separated assemblies of God's people *called out* to positively impact the atmosphere of the communities in which they live.

We are the Church — a Body of believers who have been called out, called forth, selected, and assembled to be God's representatives in every town, city, state, or nation. We are a Body called to make decisions that affect the atmosphere of every region in which we live.

Understanding Pergamum Is Key to Understanding Thyatira

Archaeologists tell us that the city of Thyatira and the surrounding region were first established by the Hittites in approximately 3,000 BC. Time passed, and in approximately 500 BC, the city came under Persian rule. Eventually the mighty military leader Alexander the Great of Greece conquered that region, and upon his death, the territory was divided among his top four generals.

Meanwhile, about 25 miles away, the illustrious city of Pergamum was erected, and it became one of the most legendary cities ever constructed in human history. It was so admired that even 1,000 years later when Roman sculptors were carving images out of marble, they attempted to duplicate the architecture of Pergamum because of its greatness.

Out of all of Asia's cities, Pergamum was the diamond. No other city compared with its overall brilliance. Consequently, aggressive thieves from the east wanted to attack and plunder Pergamum of all its treasures. To protect themselves from eastern invaders, the people of Pergamum built the ancient city of Thyatira, making it a mighty military barrier of defense.

The wealthy people of Pergamum invested copious amounts of money into Thyatira, establishing it as a major military outpost. Even though it was small and architecturally uninteresting, the city became quite affluent and served as a strong wall of protection against eastern raiders.

Trade Guilds Played a Powerful Role in Thyatira

When a newcomer arrived in Thyatira for the first time, he would have seen thousands of military tents encircling the city along with thousands of armed soldiers moving about. This was quite a different sight than what one saw in the legendary cities of Pergamum, Sardis, and Ephesus.

In addition to being a military outpost, Thyatira had a thriving commercial center, which catered to sustaining the needs of the military. Clothing businesses, animal caretakers, eating establishments, and other defense-related industries all had a strong presence in the city. With all of this commerce, Thyatira developed and became known for its many trade guilds. In fact, it had the most organized trade guilds of all cities throughout the Roman Empire in the First Century.

Trade guilds were much like unions are today. If a person was a member of a trade guild, he was virtually guaranteed work. If he was not a member, he couldn't get a job. This dominating influence became a major challenge for believers, since trade guilds were saturated with pagan practices.

At the opening of each trade-guild meeting, members would get on their knees and worship the patron god they had selected for their organization. Drunkenness, orgies, and debaucheries of all kinds were an integral part of each gathering, and every member was expected to participate.

Believers in Thyatira were faced with a very difficult decision: Remain in the trade guild in order to keep their jobs and earn a living — or honor God with their lives and truly live as the *ekklesia*, the called-out ones. To stay in a trade guild, believers would have to worship foreign gods, as well as participate in all the drunkenness and sexual immorality that came with it. Those who didn't participate in these activities had their membership revoked and were blacklisted from receiving further employment.

These details concerning trade guilds and employment are very important to understand in light of the message Christ spoke to the church of Thyatira. In our upcoming lessons, we will see how a woman named Jezebel was encouraging the local believers to compromise Christ's standards in order to keep their jobs.

STUDY QUESTIONS

> Study to shew thyself approved unto God, a workman that needeth not to be ashamed, rightly dividing the word of truth.
> — 2 Timothy 2:15

1. What new and interesting insights have you discovered about the city of Thyatira?
2. Why do you think so many pastors and teachers stay away from ministering on the topic of Christ's message to Thyatira? In your own words, tell why you believe it is vital that we hear and understand this message.

PRACTICAL APPLICATION

> But be ye doers of the word, and not hearers only, deceiving your own selves.
> — James 1:22

We are the Church (*ekklesia*) — a Body of believers who have been called out, called forth, selected, and assembled to be God's representatives in every town, city, state, and nation, making decisions that affect the very atmosphere of every region in which we live.

1. Be honest. As a member of Christ's Church, are you fulfilling this calling?
2. If so, how? What evidence confirms your effectiveness?
3. If not, take a moment to repent and ask the Holy Spirit to show you some practical steps you can take to *be* His Church (*ekklesia*) and to positively impact the world around you.

TOPIC

Intelligence and Judgment

SCRIPTURES

1. **Revelation 2:18** — And unto the angel of the church in Thyatira write; These things saith the Son of God, who hath his eyes like unto a flame of fire, and his feet are like fine brass.

GREEK WORDS

1. "angel" — ἄγγελος (*angelos*): a human messenger or angel; one sent on a special mission; one dispatched to perform a specific assignment; a delegate or dignitary; pictures the role of a pastor; a messenger of God

2. "church" — ἐκκλησία (*ekklesia*): a called, separated assembly; a prestigious assembly of distinguished citizens who determined laws, debated public policy, formulated new policies, argued and ruled in judicial matters, elected chief magistrates, and decided who should be banished; a body of believers who have been called out, called forth, selected, and assembled to be God's representatives in every town, city, state, or nation; a body called to make decisions that affect the atmosphere of a region

3. "who hath" — ἔχων (*echon*): a form of ἔχω, meaning to have; to hold; to have in one's possession

SYNOPSIS

The ruins of the ancient city of Thyatira are located in modern-day Turkey, and they are quite a remarkable sight to behold. Jesus spoke a powerful message to the church of Thyatira, and it is recorded in Revelation 2. After acknowledging many amazing things the believers were doing right, He issued a strong warning to them because they were allowing a leader in the church to teach doctrinal error. Jesus urged them to repent and remove this person from her position of influence; otherwise, He would bring judgment upon them.

The emphasis of this lesson:

What Jesus said to the church of Thyatira, He is still saying to the Church today. People who promote doctrinal error — or tolerate those who do — must repent to avoid coming under the judgment of God.

The apostle John received Christ's message to the church of Thyatira while in the Cave of the Revelation on the Isle of Patmos. In Revelation 1:10, John wrote about his experience, saying, "I was in the Spirit on the Lord's day, and heard behind me a great voice, as of a trumpet."

In our first lesson, we learned that the words "I was" is a translation of the Greek word *ginomai*, which describes *something that takes you completely off-guard or by surprise*. This phrase could literally be translated as John saying, "I don't know how this happened; I was not expecting or anticipating it. But in some strange way that I cannot explain, I suddenly found myself in the spirit on the Lord's day."

We also noted that the word "Spirit" is capitalized in the *King James Version*, but in the Greek it is lowercased. It doesn't refer to the Holy Spirit; instead, it refers to *the spirit realm*. Basically, John said, "I suddenly left the natural confines of the cave and transitioned into another dimension — the dimension of the spirit."

The voice John heard in the realm of the spirit was the voice of Jesus. The Lord instructed him to write what he heard and "…send it unto the seven churches which are in Asia; unto Ephesus, and unto Smyrna, and unto Pergamos, and unto Thyatira, and unto Sardis, and unto Philadelphia, and unto Laodicea" (Revelation 1:11).

The 'Angel' of the Church of Thyatira

The fourth church Christ addressed was the church of Thyatira. In Revelation 2:18, Jesus said, "And unto the angel of the church in Thyatira write; These things saith the Son of God, who hath his eyes like unto a flame of fire, and his feet are like fine brass."

Notice again the word "angel." It is the Greek word *angelos*, which describes *a human messenger or angel; one sent on a special mission; one dispatched to perform a specific assignment*; or *a delegate or dignitary*. Although the word *angelos* can describe a heavenly being, in this verse it pictures the role of the pastor of the church of Thyatira.

When Jesus wants to speak to His Church, He doesn't send an angel to do it. It is not angels' responsibility to teach doctrine or bring correction to His people. The fact is, most of the false doctrine that was being taught during the time of the Early Church purportedly came from the teachings of angels. If you hear of anyone who has received a new teaching from an angel, don't listen to a word he or she says; it is not of God.

Jesus has gifted His Church with pastors, evangelists, teachers, apostles, and prophets to be His messengers (*see* Ephesians 4:10,11). And pastors are the ones Christ has placed in authority over the local churches. When He has something to say to a church, He is going to speak it to the pastor first. The word *angelos* — translated here as "angel" — indicates that pastors are like angels, bringing His Word to His people.

The Meaning of the Word 'Church'

The word "church" in Revelation 2:18 is also very significant. It is the Greek word *ekklesia*, and it is used throughout the New Testament. The word *ekklesia* is a compound of the word *ek*, which means *out*, and a derivative of the word *kaleo*, which means *to call* or *to summon*. When the two words are joined to form the word *ekklesia*, the new word describes *those who have been summoned or called out*.

The word *ekklesia* was not originally a New Testament word. It was a secular word borrowed from the Athenian culture. It was used to describe certain people in Athens that were *a called, separated, and prestigious assembly of distinguished citizens who determined laws, debated public policy, formulated new policies, argued and ruled in judicial matters, elected chief magistrates, and decided who should be banished.*

When the New Testament writers began to describe God's people in the local assembly, they intelligently chose the word *ekklesia*. The "church" is *a body of believers who have been called out, called forth, selected, and assembled to be God's representatives in every town, city, state, or nation.* By using this word, God's leaders were saying, "We are the ones called forth out of society by God to make decisions that affect the atmosphere of every region where we live. We take actions in the spirit realm that produce positive changes everywhere." This is what it means to be Christ's Church (*ekklesia*). We are His called-out ones invested with power and authority to bring God's will on earth as it is in Heaven.

Jesus' Eyes Burned Like 'Fire'

When Jesus spoke His message to the pastor of the church of Thyatira, it is important to note how John described His appearance. Revelation 2:18 says, "…These things saith the Son of God, who hath his eyes like unto a flame of fire, and his feet are like fine brass."

First, notice the phrase "who hath." It is the Greek word *echon*, meaning *to have, to hold, or to have in one's possession*. Jesus is the One who possesses eyes like fire and feet like fine brass. It's interesting to note that this is the same imagery and Greek wording used in Revelation 1:14 and 15 to describe Christ — having eyes like fire and feet like fine brass.

The words "his eyes" in Greek carry a deep sense of wonder. They imply that there was something very unique and different about Jesus' eyes compared to everyone else's eyes. Jesus' eyes were matchless in comparison. Although John had looked into Jesus' eyes countless times nearly 60 years earlier during Christ's earthly ministry, something was now markedly different. Jesus' eyes were compelling, riveting, and magnetic, irresistibly drawing John closer and closer to Him.

This leads us to the words "flame of fire." The word "fire" is the Greek word *puris*, which describes *a blazing fire*. The phrase "flame of fire" depicts *a brightly burning fire with flames that are swirling, whirling, bending, twisting, turning and arching upward toward the sky*. It is not describing the heat of the fire, but the *character* of the fire.

One more important aspect for us to understand is the purpose for fire. In Scripture, fire was used to purify or to destroy. The fact that Jesus was coming to the church of Thyatira with fire in His eyes indicates His desire to purify them of their impurities. But if they refused to cooperate with His purification, that same fire would bring judgment upon them.

Jesus' Feet Were Like 'Fine Brass'

In addition to Jesus' eyes being like a flame of fire, the Bible says His feet were like "fine brass." The phrase "fine brass" is the Greek word *chalkolibano* — a compound of the word *chalkos*, meaning *brass or bronze*, and the word *libanos*, meaning *frankincense*. In this verse, brass and frankincense are pictured as alloys attempting to be mixed together. Brass or bronze (*chalkos*) always represents *judgment*, and frankincense (*libanos*) represents *prayer* because it was the perfumed incense used by the high priest in the Holy of Holies when he made intercession for the people of Israel.

The Greek word *chalkolibano* — translated in this verse as "fine brass" — reveals that *while Christ's feet were prepared to move toward judgment, they were drenched in intercessory prayer that repentance would occur before He arrived to apply judgment.* As Jesus moved toward the church of Thyatira, His eyes were deeply examining all that was taking place inside the church. The fire in His eyes was meant to purify them, if only they would turn and repent of their sin. This is what He was praying would happen. His judgment was coming, but it was bathed in prayer.

There is something else about brass that is very important, and that is its *weight.* Brass is extremely heavy. Thus, when the Bible says that Jesus' feet are like "brass" (*chalkos*), it indicates that *He is not moving very fast.* In fact, with feet of brass, He is moving very slowly. In other words, Jesus was not rushing to judgment against the believers in Thyatira. Yes, He was coming with divine correction, but His judgment was very slow in coming and saturated with much prayer.

The same is true of Jesus today. He is not in a rush to judge anyone; that is His last resort. He gives people space to repent — just as He did with Jezebel, who was contaminating the church of Thyatira. Jesus is praying for people to hear His voice and self-correct — to repent and turn from their path of sin and selfishness. He longs for them to change *before* He must deal sternly with them.

STUDY QUESTIONS

Study to shew thyself approved unto God, a workman that needeth not to be ashamed, rightly dividing the word of truth.
— 2 Timothy 2:15

1. Jesus gave Jezebel time to repent and make things right (*see* Revelation 2:21). According to Psalm 103:12 and First John 1:9, what can you expect the Lord to do when you sincerely repent of any sin you've committed?

2. The teaching and preaching of God's Word, as well as administering His correction, is to be carried out by humans, not angels. What did Paul say in Galatians 1:6-9 about those who present a gospel that is

different than the original one? (Also consider Proverbs 30:5,6; Revelation 22:18,19.)

3. The imagery of Jesus' feet being made of "fine brass" indicates *His judgment is slow in coming and bathed in prayer*. He is not in a rush to judge you or anyone else. What do Second Peter 3:9 and Ezekiel 18:23 say that confirm this to be true? How does this understanding tweak your perspective of Jesus' judgment?

PRACTICAL APPLICATION

> But be ye doers of the word, and not hearers only,
> deceiving your own selves.
> — James 1:22

1. A careful reading of Jesus' messages to each of the seven churches in Revelation 2 and 3 reveals that before He brought correction, He first brought praise for what the believers were doing right. Why do you think it is so vital to couple praise with correction?

2. When you bring correction to those under your care, do you also point out the good they are doing and the progress they have made? If not, why not?

3. If someone corrected you in the exact manner that you correct others, how would you respond? What would you change about their manner of correction?

LESSON 3

TOPIC
A Church Committed to Good Works

SCRIPTURES

1. **Revelation 2:18,19** — And unto the angel of the church in Thyatira write; These things saith the Son of God, who hath his eyes like unto a flame of fire, and his feet are like fine brass. I know thy works, and charity, and service, and faith, and thy patience, and thy works; and the last to be more than the first.

GREEK WORDS

1. "who hath" — ἔχων (*echon*): a form of ἔχω, meaning to have, to hold, to have in one's possession

2. "flame of fire" — the word "flame" pictures the swirling, whirling, flickering flames that bend, twist, turn, and arch upward; the word "fire" depicts brightly burning fire with flames swirling, whirling, flickering, bending, twisting, turning, and arching upward toward the sky; not a depiction of heat, but of the character of fire

3. "fine brass" — χαλκολιβάνῳ (*chalkolibano*): a compound of χαλκός (*chalkos*), meaning brass or bronze, representing judgment, and λίβανος (*libanos*), meaning frankincense, representing prayer; when combined, the new word reveals that although Christ's feet are prepared to move toward judgment, they are doused in intercessory prayer that repentance will occur before He arrives to apply judgment

4. "I know" — οἶδα (*oida*): to see, perceive, understand, or comprehend; pictures knowledge gained by personal experience or personal observation

5. "works" — ἔργα (*erga*): deeds, actions, or activities

6. "charity" — τὴν ἀγάπη (*ten agapen*): with a definite article, a love that gives and gives, even if it's never responded to, thanked, or acknowledged; a love felt when an individual sees, recognizes, or appreciates the value of an object or a person; a deep love that causes a viewer to behold an object or person in esteem, awe, admiration, wonder, and sincere appreciation; a love so profound that it knows no limits or boundaries in how far, wide, high, and deep it will go to show that love to its recipient; a self-sacrificial love that moves one to action

7. "service" — τὴν διακονίαν (*ten diakonian*): with a definite article, a high-level servant; highly trained servants who attended to the needs of others; a servant whose chief responsibility was to serve food and wait on tables; a waiter who attends to the needs, wishes, and desires of his or her clients; pictures serving that is honorable, pleasurable, and done in a fashion that makes people being served as if they were nobility

8. "faith" — τὴν πίστιν (*ten pisten*): with a definite article, denotes a specific set of beliefs, a specific creed, or a specific faith; refers to the faith, or the body of truth comprising the New Testament

9. "patience" — **τὴν ὑπομονήν σου** (*ten hupomonen sou*): a form of **ὑπομονή** (*hupomone*) to stay or to abide; to remain in one's spot; to keep a position; to resolve to maintain territory that has been gained; in a military sense, pictures soldiers who were ordered to maintain their positions even in the face of fierce combat; to defiantly stick it out, regardless of the pressure mounted against it; endurance; staying power; "hang-in-there" power; the attitude that holds out, holds on, outlasts, perseveres, and hangs in there, never giving up, refusing to surrender to obstacles, and turning down every opportunity to quit; pictures one who is under a heavy load but refuses to bend, break, or surrender because he is convinced that the territory, promise, or principle under assault rightfully belongs to him; stamina; durability

10. "thy works" — **ἔργα** (*erga*): deeds, actions, or activities

11. "the last" — **ἔσχατα** (*eschata*): the latest, or the most recent

12. "more than" — **πλείων** (*pleion*): comparatively more; numerically more

13. "the first" — **πρώτων** (*proton*): the first; the beginning; at the start

SYNOPSIS

The city of Pergamum was very rich in resources and financial means. It was home not only to the affluent, but also to many politicians and even the governor of the region. To protect their city, the people of Pergamum built the city of Thyatira approximately 40 kilometers (25 miles) to the east. It served as a military outpost to guard against eastern invaders who wanted to attack and plunder it.

When the first Gospel preachers traveled to Thyatira, they were very bold and unashamed in sharing their faith. The city was very dark spiritually and entrenched in multiple pagan religions. Yet when theses believers presented the truth, the Gospel did what it always does — it drove back the powers of darkness, and the Church of the Lord Jesus Christ was established.

There were a number of good works for which Jesus commended the church of Thyatira. He deeply appreciated their love, faith, service, and perseverance to advance His Kingdom. Although He did address their shortcomings, He first expressed His praise for all the great things they were doing in the community.

The emphasis of this lesson:

The way Jesus dealt with the church of Thyatira demonstrates that He sees and takes note of our good works. Before He brings correction, He always praises what we're doing right.

During John's time of imprisonment on the Isle of Patmos, the Lord unexpectedly invaded John's space and vividly revealed Himself. He also gave John seven specific messages to relay to the seven major churches in Asia. In Revelation 1:10, John said, "I was in the Spirit on the Lord's day, and heard behind me a great voice, as of a trumpet."

As we previously noted, the words "I was" is the Greek word *ginomai*, and it describes *something unanticipated that takes you totally off guard or by surprise*. This phrase could literally be translated, "Suddenly, something happened in a way I cannot explain or duplicate. Without notice, I found myself moving out of the natural realm into the supernatural realm of the spirit. It was then that I heard a great voice behind me that sounded like a trumpet."

At that point, Jesus began speaking to John, giving him a specific message for each of the seven major churches, starting with the church of Ephesus, followed by the church of Smyrna, the church of Pergamum, and, fourthly, the church of Thyatira.

The Fire in Jesus' Eyes Is Meant To Purify

In Revelation 2:18, Jesus said, "And unto the angel of the church in Thyatira write; These things saith the Son of God, who hath his eyes like unto a flame of fire, and his feet are like fine brass."

Notice the words "who hath" in this verse. It is the Greek word *echon*, which means *to have, to hold*, or *to have in one's possession*. Jesus had in His possession "eyes like unto a flame of fire." The word "flame" in the Greek is the word *flus*, and it *pictures the swirling, whirling, flickering flames that bend, twist, turn, and arch upward*. The word "fire" is the Greek word *puris*, and it depicts *brightly burning fire with flames swirling, whirling, flickering, bending, twisting, turning, and arching upward toward the sky*. This is not a depiction of heat, but of *the character of fire*.

When you stare into the flames of a blazing fire, it seems to have a life of its own. It moves with deliberateness and intelligence. It has a riveting magnetism that pulls and compels the viewer to draw closer and continue to gaze at it. This is what happened to the apostle John when he looked into the eyes of Christ.

In the New Testament, fire is a symbol of purification. The fact that Jesus had "fire" in His eyes as He moved toward the church of Thyatira indicates His desire to purify the believers of that congregation with His words of truth. If the people chose not to respond favorably, however, that same fire would begin to burn up all the things that were not of Him.

The same is true for us. If we will humbly and willingly submit to the correction of the Lord, His fire will gently purify us. But if we reject His correction and refuse to yield to His dealings, His fire will burn up the chaff in our lives, and the process will be more painful. Either way, He purifies us in love. The choice is ours.

Jesus' Judgment Is Bathed in Prayer

In addition to having "eyes like unto a flame of fire," Jesus also held in His possession "feet like fine brass." The words "fine brass" is the Greek word *chalkolibano*. It is a compound of the words *chalkos*, which describes *bronze or brass*, and the word *libanos*, which describes *frankincense*. When the word *chalkos* is used in Scripture, it signifies God's judgment. The fact that Jesus is depicted with "feet of brass" (*chalkos*) indicates that He was coming to the church in Thyatira to bring judgment.

That said, it is also vital to understand what the word *libanos*, which describes *frankincense*, indicates. In the New Testament — as well as in the Septuagint, the Greek translation of the Old Testament — frankincense represents *intercessory prayer*. The high priest burned frankincense upon the altar when he entered the Holy of Holies to pray and seek God's favor on behalf of the people. The aroma of frankincense was a sweet smell to the Lord.

When the words *chalkos* and *libanos* are compounded to form the word *chalkolibano* — translated here as "fine brass" — it is a picture of *God's judgment mixed with divine prayer*. It reveals that although Christ's feet are prepared to move toward judgment, they are doused in intercessory prayer that repentance will occur before He arrives to apply that judgment. This word is used only once in the New Testament.

One more detail we noted is that brass is extremely heavy. The fact that Jesus' feet are depicted as brass indicates He was moving very slowly.

This means that although judgment was on the way, Jesus was not in a rush to bring it. When He spoke to the church of Thyatira, He didn't say, "I'm coming to destroy you immediately." On the contrary, He issued His warning and gave them and the woman Jezebel time to repent (*see* Revelation 2:21).

As the Lord slowly moves to bring judgment, He is praying that the people will hear His message and repent before He arrives.

As you deal with people who are doing wrong things, give them time to self-correct. Don't be hasty, haughty, or severe in your actions. Pray for them to hear and heed your words and make things right. That is what Jesus does for you, and it is what He desires you to do for others.

Jesus Is Personally Aware of Our Works

Jesus continued His message to the church of Thyatira saying, "I know thy works, and charity, and service, and faith, and thy patience, and thy works; and the last to be more than the first" (Revelation 2:19).

Notice the phrase that introduces this verse — "I know." It is the same phrase Jesus spoke to all seven churches. The words "I know" is the Greek word *oida*, which means *to know from personal experience or observation*. By using this word, it was the equivalent of Jesus saying, "What I'm about to tell you is what I've seen with My own eyes and what I know by personal experience."

The Lord confirms this firsthand observation of His Church in Revelation 2:1, declaring that He walks in the very midst or the "gut" of each of the churches. Still today He visits every church — small, medium, and large — and is intimately mindful of all that is happening. What did Jesus say He knew by personal observation about the church of Thyatira? He said, "I know thy *works*."

The word "works" is the Greek word *erga*, which describes *deeds, actions*, or *activities*. When Jesus said, "I know thy works," it was the equivalent of Him saying, "I intimately know everything about you, and there is absolutely nothing about you I do not know."

The same is true of us today. Jesus knows everything about each church and about each of us individually.

What Gets the Attention of Jesus?

The first attribute of the church of Thyatira that Jesus praised was their works of "charity," which is the Greek word *agape*. In this verse, *agape* is coupled with a definite article (*ten agapen*). It describes *a love that gives and gives, even if it's never responded to, thanked, or acknowledged; a love felt when an individual sees, recognizes, or appreciates the value of an object or a person; a deep love that causes a viewer to behold an object or person in esteem, awe, admiration, wonder, and sincere appreciation; a love so profound that it knows no limits or boundaries in how far, wide, high, and deep it will go to show that love to its recipient; a self-sacrificial love that moves one to action.*

The next quality for which Jesus commended the believers at Thyatira was "service," which is the Greek word *diakonian*. Like *agape*, the word "service" (*diakonian*) includes a definite article (*ten diakonian*). This means that Thyatira's service was very unique to them. The word *diakonian* depicts *a high-level servant* or *highly trained servants who attended to the needs of others.* Specifically, this describes *a servant whose chief responsibility was to serve food and wait on tables; a waiter who attends to the needs, wishes, and desires of his or her clients.* It pictures *serving that is honorable, pleasurable, and done in a fashion that makes people being served feel as if they were nobility.*

Jesus also applauded the church of Thyatira for their "faith." Again, this was not just any faith — it was "the faith," which in Greek is *ten pisten*. By including a definite article, it denotes *a specific set of beliefs, a specific creed,* or *a specific faith.* It refers to *the faith,* or to *the body of truth comprising the New Testament.*

In addition to charity, service, and faith, Jesus recognized the "patience" of these believers. The word "patience" in this verse is the Greek phrase *ten hupomonen sou.* It is a form of the word *hupomone*, which means *to stay or to abide; to remain in one's spot; to keep a position; to resolve to maintain territory that has been gained.* In a military sense, the word *hupomone* pictures soldiers who were ordered to maintain their positions even in the face of fierce combat. It means *to defiantly stick it out regardless of the pressure mounted against it.* It describes *endurance; staying power; "hang-in-there" power; the attitude that holds out, holds on, outlasts, perseveres, and hangs in there, never giving up, refusing to surrender to obstacles, and turning down every opportunity to quit.* It pictures one who is under a heavy load but *refuses to bend, break, or surrender* because he is convinced that the territory, promise, or principle under assault rightfully belongs to him. "Patience" (*hupomone*) means *stamina* or *durability*.

Even Great Churches Can Be Derailed

As Jesus walked in the midst of the church of Thyatira, He personally observed their unique display of love, their high-level acts of service to others, their rich Bible teaching grounded in the faith, and their unwavering patience to stand their ground in spite of great challenges. For all these things, He commended them. Then for a second time, Jesus noted and praised their "works," which is the Greek word *erga*, meaning *deeds, actions,* or *activities*. This was the equivalent of Jesus saying, "I'm impressed with everything you're doing."

In fact, Jesus said concerning their works, "…And the last to be more than the first" (Revelation 2:19). The phrase "the last" is the Greek word *eschata*, which means *the latest* or *the most recent*. The phrase "more than" is the Greek word *pleion*, which means *comparatively more* or *numerically more*. And the words "the first" in Greek is the word *proton*, which describes *the first, the beginning,* or *at the start*. When all these meanings are woven together, this part of the verse could be translated, "The level of all your most recent deeds and activities is far greater in comparison to what you did when you first got saved."

Indeed, Thyatira was truly an amazing body of believers. Their commitment to excellence in all areas of Christian life just kept getting better and better and better, and Jesus celebrated their maturity and the impact they were making on their community. Yet in the midst of all their success, there was something very disturbing that they were permitting, and it was about to derail them if they didn't address it.

STUDY QUESTIONS

Study to shew thyself approved unto God, a workman that needeth not to be ashamed, rightly dividing the word of truth.
— 2 Timothy 2:15

1. What recurring truth about God's character is seen in Hebrews 4:13; First John 3:20; and Jeremiah 32:19? (Also consider Psalm 139:1-6,16.)

2. How does the Bible say that patience is developed in you? What value does this quality add to your life? (*See* James 1:3,4; 5:7,8 and Hebrews 10:36 for help in answering.)

PRACTICAL APPLICATION

> **But be ye doers of the word, and not hearers only,
> deceiving your own selves.**
> **— James 1:22**

1. Take a few moments to reread and ponder the meaning of *hupomone*, the Greek word for *patience*. In what areas of your life can you see this fruit at work? In what areas do you still need the Holy Spirit to develop patience in you?
2. Jesus said, "In everything, do to others what you would have them do to you…" (Matthew 7:12 *NIV*). The Lord is incredibly patient and merciful in bringing correction to you. How would you describe your correction of those under your care?

LESSON 4

TOPIC

Who Is Jezebel?

SCRIPTURES

1. **Revelation 2:18-20** — And unto the angel of the church in Thyatira write; These things saith the Son of God, who hath his eyes like unto a flame of fire, and his feet are like fine brass. I know thy works, and charity, and service, and faith, and thy patience, and thy works; and the last to be more than the first. Notwithstanding I have a few things against thee, because thou sufferest that woman Jezebel, which calleth herself a prophetess, to teach and to seduce my servants to commit fornication, and to eat things sacrificed unto idols.

GREEK WORDS

1. "I know" — οἶδα (*oida*): to see, to perceive, to understand, or to comprehend; pictures knowledge gained by personal experience or personal observation

2. "works" — ἔργα (*erga*): deeds, actions, or activities

3. "charity" — τὴν ἀγάπη (*ten agapen*): with a definite article, a love that gives and gives, even if it's never responded to, thanked, or acknowledged; a love felt when an individual sees, recognizes, or appreciates the value of an object or a person; a deep love that causes a viewer to behold an object or person in esteem, awe, admiration, wonder, and sincere appreciation; a love so profound that it knows no limits or boundaries in how far, wide, high, and deep it will go to show that love to its recipient; a self-sacrificial love that moves one to action

4. "service" — τὴν διακονίαν (*ten diakonian*): with a definite article, a high-level servant; highly trained servants who attended to the needs of others; a servant whose chief responsibility was to serve food and wait on tables; a waiter who attends to the needs, wishes, and desires of his or her clients; pictures serving that is honorable, pleasurable, and done in a fashion that makes people being served feel as if they were nobility

5. "faith" — τὴν πίστιν (*ten pisten*): with a definite article, denotes a specific set of beliefs, a specific, a specific creed, or a specific faith; refers to the faith, or the body of truth comprising the New Testament

6. "thy patience" — τὴν ὑπομονήν σου (*ten hupomonen sou*): as "patience," a form of ὑπομονή (*hupomone*) to stay or to abide; to remain in one's spot; to keep a position; to resolve to maintain territory that has been gained; in a military sense, pictures soldiers who were ordered to maintain their positions even in the face of fierce combat; to defiantly stick it out, regardless of the pressure mounted against it; endurance; staying power; "hang-in-there" power; the attitude that holds out, holds on, outlasts, perseveres, and hangs in there, never giving up, refusing to surrender to obstacles, and turning down every opportunity to quit; pictures one who is under a heavy load but refuses to bend, break, or surrender because he is convinced that the territory, promise, or principle under assault rightfully belongs to him; stamina; durability

7. "thy works" — ἔργα (*erga*): deeds, actions, or activities

8. "more than" — πλείων (*pleion*): comparatively more; numerically more
9. "the first" — πρώτων (*proton*): the first; the beginning; at the start
10. "notwithstanding" — ἀλλὰ (*alla*): nonetheless; regardless; but even in spite of this
11. "I have" — ἔχω (*echo*): to hold or to embrace; to hold something very personally
12. "against" — κατὰ (*kata*): against; down; a strike against you
13. "because" — ὅτι (*hoti*): indicates expressly the reason
14. "sufferest" — ἀφίημι (*aphiemi*): to permit, to release; to let go; to liberate; to give unrestrained freedom
15. "that woman" — τὴν γυναῖκα (*ten gunaika*): with a definite article, the woman, indicating a woman of prominence; the two oldest man-uscripts say "your wife," giving the strong impression that this Jezebel was the wife of the pastor in Thyatira
16. "a prophetess" — προφήτης (*prophetes*): a compound of the words πρό (*pro*) and φημί (*phemi*), meaning an interpreter or forth-teller of the divine will
17. "to seduce" — πλανάω (*planao*): deception; a moral wandering; depicts a person or nation that has veered from a solid path; as a result of veering morally, that person or nation is adrift; depicts a lost animal that cannot find its path; to morally lose one's bearings
18. "to commit fornication" — πορνεία (*porneia*): any type of sex with another person outside the bond of marriage; includes sexual activity by non-married individuals; includes both adultery and homosexuality

SYNOPSIS

About 2,000 years ago, the city of Thyatira was a small but thriving city located just east of the city of Pergamum. It was constructed to serve as a military outpost to protect Pergamum and all its vast wealth. As a military stronghold, Thyatira was occupied by thousands of soldiers, troops, and their many commanding officers, as well as by many politicians. Into this region inhabited by rough men and exotic religions, bold believers brought the Gospel and established a powerful church that shined a great light in the midst of gross darkness.

Yet despite her great deeds, the church of Thyatira had a big problem. It was allowing a woman in the church to teach doctrine that was seducing believers and leading them into sexual sin. Jesus called this woman Jezebel, connecting her with the notorious Jezebel of the Old Testament. His stern warning and words of correction to the church of Thyatira are just as applicable to us today as they were when He first spoke them.

The emphasis of this lesson:

Jesus hates compromise. It diminishes the power of God and removes holiness from our lives. Just as He loved the believers at Thyatira enough to correct them, He loves you enough to correct you.

The church of Thyatira was the fourth of seven churches that Jesus spoke a specific message to in Revelation chapters 2 and 3. The apostle John received Christ's words of praise and correction while on the isle of Patmos. In Revelation 2:18, Jesus told John, "And unto the angel of the church in Thyatira write; These things saith the Son of God, who hath his eyes like unto a flame of fire, and his feet are like fine brass."

We've learned that the word "angel" is the Greek word *angelos*. Although this Greek word can and sometimes does refer to a heavenly being, here it refers to *a human messenger*. Specifically, in Revelation 2:18-29, Jesus was speaking to *the pastor* of the church in Thyatira.

Pastors are God's appointed representatives who oversee specific local works within His Church. If He has something to say to His people, He honors the spiritual authority He has established and speaks to His pastors first. It is the pastor's job to assimilate the Lord's message, apply it to his life first, and then deliver it to the people under his care in the power of the Holy Spirit.

Jesus First Commended Thyatira

In our last lesson, we looked at Jesus' words of praise for the believers in Thyatira in Revelation 2:19. He said, "I know thy works, and charity, and service, and faith, and thy patience, and thy works; and the last to be more than the first." Here is a quick review of the key words in this verse.

Jesus began by saying, "I know thy works." The phrase "I know" is the Greek word *oida*, which means *to see, to perceive, to understand*, or *to comprehend*. It pictures *knowledge gained by personal experience or personal observation*. From the start, Jesus told the pastor of Thyatira, through John, that what He was about to say regarding this congregation was a result of personal observation. It wasn't something an angel or anyone else told Him.

"I know thy works," Jesus announced. The word "works" is the Greek word *erga*, which describes *deeds, actions*, or *activities*. Essentially, Jesus was saying, "I know absolutely everything there is to know about you, and I have seen it by personal observation. There is nothing hidden from My sight."

Jesus praised the believers for their "charity." The word "charity" is from the Greek word *agape*. This is one of the most difficult words in the New Testament to fully translate as it is packed with so much meaning. In this verse, the word *agape* is accompanied by a definite article (*ten agapen*), and it describes *a love that gives and gives, even if it's never responded to, thanked, or acknowledged*. It is *a love so profound that it knows no limits or boundaries in how far, wide, high, and deep it will go to show that love to its recipient.*

An example of God's *agape* kind of love is displayed in John 3:16, which says, "For God so loved the world, that he gave his only begotten Son...." This verse indicates that when God saw all of humanity — all of whom are made in His image — it created such an intense love and appreciation in His heart that He had to take action to redeem man. The word *agape* denotes *a self-sacrificial love that moves one to action.* That is what we see God doing in John 3:16 — and the believers of the church in Thyatira doing in Revelation 2.

Jesus applauded the believers for their "service." The word "service" is the Greek word *diakonian*, and it really means *ministry*. Again, a definite article is included, which means we would translate this as "the service" or "the ministry" (*ten diakonian*). The word *diakonian* described *a very high-level of service/ministry*. The church of Thyatira had a reputation for doing things with excellence. The word *diakonian* is a picture of *highly trained servants who attended to the needs of others*. It depicts *serving that is honorable, pleasurable, and done in a fashion that makes people being served feel as if they were nobility.*

Jesus commended the believers for their "faith." The word "faith" in Greek is the word *pisteo*, and here again a definite article is included. This is not just faith for miracles, faith for signs and wonders, or faith for healing. It is "the faith" (*ten pisten*), which denotes *a specific set of beliefs, a specific creed*, or *a specific faith*. It refers to *the faith* or *the body of truth comprising the New Testament*. Thyatira had very strong scriptural teaching, and Jesus recognized it.

Jesus praised the believers for their "patience." The word "patience" is from the Greek word *hupomone*, which means *to stay or to abide*; *to remain in one's spot*; *to keep a position*; or *to resolve to maintain territory that has been gained*. It is *the attitude that holds out, holds on, outlasts, perseveres, and hangs in there, never giving up, refusing to surrender to obstacles, and turning down every opportunity to quit*. As with charity, service, and faith, the word "patience" is also accompanied by a definite article and could be translated as "the patience of you." This indicates that in comparison to everyone else, the church of Thyatira had amazing *stamina, endurance*, or *staying power*.

Jesus summed up His commendations for the believers in Thyatira by reiterating the superior quality of their "works," adding that He recognized "…the last to be more than the first." The word "works" here is again the Greek word *erga*, meaning *all deeds, actions, and activities*. The phrase "the last" is the Greek word *eschata*, which denotes *the latest* or *the most recent*. The phrase "more than" is the Greek word *pleion*, and it means *comparatively more* or *numerically more*. And the phrase "the first" in Greek is the word *proton*, which describes *the first, the beginning*, or *at the start*. When we combine all these meanings, this part of the verse could be translated, "The quality of all your most recent deeds and activities is far superior when compared to what you did when you first began."

Thyatira Had a Strike Against Them

Once Jesus commended the church of Thyatira for all their good deeds, He turned His attention to correcting a glaring issue that desperately needed to be addressed. In Revelation 2:20, He said, "Notwithstanding I have a few things against thee, because thou sufferest that woman Jezebel, which calleth herself a prophetess, to teach and to seduce my servants to commit fornication, and to eat things sacrificed unto idols."

First, notice the word "notwithstanding." It is the Greek word *alla*, which is basically a break in the text or a brief pause noting a transition to another topic or a different direction. It means *nonetheless; regardless; but even in spite of all this*. When Jesus said, "Notwithstanding (*alla*)," He was saying, "Let's take a pause and transition to something I need to deal with. In spite of all the amazing things you have done and are doing, I have a few things against you."

The phrase "I have" is a form of the Greek word *echo*, which means *to hold*; *to embrace*; or *to hold something very personally*. This tells us that what Jesus was about ready to address was a matter He held very personally and He found deeply disturbing.

Jesus said, "I have a few things against thee." The word "against" is the Greek word *kata*, which means *against; down*; or *a strike against someone*. Taken together, the first portion of verse 20 could be translated as, "In spite of all the marvelous things I've said about you, there is an issue we need to deal with. In fact, it is a strike against you that is personally very disturbing to Me."

Jezebel Was Given Free Rein in the Church of Thyatira

What was the strike against the church in Thyatira? Jesus said, "…Because thou sufferest that woman Jezebel, which calleth herself a prophetess, to teach and to seduce my servants to commit fornication, and to eat things sacrificed unto idols" (Revelation 2:20).

Interestingly, even the word "because" has significance. It is the Greek word *hoti*, and it indicates *expressly the reason or purpose*. In other words, Jesus said, "I'm going to tell you exactly why I'm upset — I'm going to be expressly clear about the strike I'm holding against you. It is '…because thou sufferest that woman Jezebel, which calleth herself a prophetess, to teach and to seduce my servants to commit fornication, and to eat things sacrificed unto idols.'"

The word "sufferest" in Greek is a form of the word *aphiemi*, which means *to permit, to release, to let go, to liberate*, or *to give unrestrained freedom*. The use of this word is the equivalent of Jesus saying, "No one has restrained or controlled this woman named Jezebel. She has been given free rein in the church to say and do whatever she pleases."

Something else significant in this verse is the phrase "that woman." The two earliest manuscripts of the New Testament state this verse a little differently. Instead of saying "that woman," these manuscripts state, "that woman of yours." In the Greek, it literally means, "your wife Jezebel." Remember, Jesus was speaking to *the pastor* of the church of Thyatira. Since He was speaking to the pastor, when He said, "that woman of yours," He was explicitly referring to the pastor's wife as the very prominent woman in the church acting like Jezebel.

To be very clear — not all pastors' wives are like Jezebel! Pastor's wives are heroes for their personal sacrifice and service. But in this case, the pastor of the church of Thyatira had a problem, and the problem was his wife. Just as King Ahab in the Old Testament didn't know how to control his wife Jezebel, neither did this pastor. The unrestrained, free rein the pastor was giving this woman to teach and say whatever she desired was the strike against the church that Jesus held very personally.

She Was Seducing People To Commit Fornication

The woman of prominence in the church of Thyatira that Jesus referred to as "Jezebel" called herself a prophetess. The word "prophetess" is the Greek word *prophetes*, which is a compound of the words *pro* and *phemi*. The word *phemi* means *to speak*, and the word *pro* has four different meanings: *before, in front of, on behalf of*, and *in advance*. These four meanings describe the various postures of a prophet.

A prophet stands *before* God and listens; he stands *in front of* people and speaks *on behalf of* God; and he tells them *in advance* what is going to take place. When the words *pro* and *phemi* are compounded to form the word *prophetes*, the new word means *an interpreter or forth-teller of the divine will*.

This woman, whom Scripture identifies as the pastor's wife, was claiming to be a prophetess, but Jesus called her Jezebel. He said she was being allowed "...to teach and to seduce [His] servants to commit fornication, and to eat things sacrificed unto idols." The problem wasn't that she was teaching; the problem was that she was *teaching error* and *abusing her position of influence*.

The phrase "to seduce" is the Greek word *planao*, and it describes *deception* or *a moral wandering*. It depicts *a person or nation who has veered from a solid path*. And as a result of veering morally, that person or nation is *adrift*. The word *planao* is the same word used to depict *a lost animal that cannot find its way back home*.

This woman of prominence was seducing the people "to commit fornication" and eat things sacrificed to idols. The phrase "to commit fornication" is the Greek word *porneia*, and it describes *any type of sex with another person outside the bond of marriage*. It refers to *sexual activity by non-married individuals, including both adultery and homosexuality*.

Jezebel Was Teaching a Doctrine of Compromise

Recall what we learned in our first lesson regarding the dominance of trade guilds in the city of Thyatira. Each guild had a patron pagan god that was worshiped by all its members. At the start of each meeting, members would offer sacrifices to their god, eat the sacrificial foods, and then engage in drunkenness and all types of fornication, including orgies. Any member who refused to participate in the club's activities had his membership revoked and was blacklisted. This is exactly what happened when believers chose not to join in the guild's pagan practices. Any person who was not a member of a trade guild was basically out of a job.

Apparently, this "Jezebel" was teaching a doctrine of compromise, which was the same doctrine the Nicolaitans were teaching in the church of Ephesus (*see* Ephesians 2:6) and in the church of Pergamum (*see* Revelation 2:15). Jesus had already brought correction to the pastors of these respective churches, and now He was dealing with the same issue in Thyatira.

Essentially, the doctrine of compromise that Jezebel was teaching declared, "It's okay to lower your standards. You don't have to live such a restrictive, separate lifestyle. Relax and learn to be more inclusive and accommodating of other people's practices. You'll blend in and gain more acceptance by people in the world."

Compromising God's standards pulls the plug on His power and removes holiness from His people. Jezebel was grieving the Spirit of God by influencing the believers of Thyatira to blend in with the world by committing fornication and eating food sacrificed to idols. God gave her time to repent, but she didn't respond to His dealings. If you are compromising God's standards to accommodate the world, it's time to repent and make things right with Him.

STUDY QUESTIONS

**Study to shew thyself approved unto God, a workman that needeth not to be ashamed, rightly dividing the word of truth.
— 2 Timothy 2:15**

God gives us a very clear command through the apostle Paul in Second Corinthians 6:14-18 to help us avoid falling into the same error of the church in Thyatira. Take a few minutes to reflect on this passage and answer these questions.

1. What specifically is God directing you to do in these verses?
2. What reasons does He give for taking such action?
3. What reward does He promise you for obeying His instruction?

PRACTICAL APPLICATION

> But be ye doers of the word, and not hearers only,
> deceiving your own selves.
> —James 1:22

1. To compromise God's standards is to know what He requires but to choose to live *below* what He commands. Be honest. Is there any place in your life where you are compromising? If so, where? (If you're not sure, ask the Lord to show you anything you need to see.)

2. Pause and pray, "Lord, please forgive me for compromising in this area of my life. I don't want to disobey You any longer. Show me the reason I've chosen to live below Your standards, and give me the practical steps I need to take to walk in obedience to Your Word. In Jesus' name." Be still and listen. What is the Holy Spirit speaking to you?

LESSON 5

TOPIC

What About Ahab?

SCRIPTURES

1. **Revelation 2:20** — Notwithstanding I have a few things against thee, because thou sufferest that woman Jezebel, which calleth herself a prophetess, to teach and to seduce my servants to commit fornication, and to eat things sacrificed unto idols.

2. **2 Kings 9:22,30** — "whoredoms ... and... her witchcrafts"

3. **1 Kings 21:25** — But there was none like unto Ahab, which did sell himself to work wickedness in the sight of the Lord, whom Jezebel his wife stirred up.

4. **2 Kings 9:30, 33-37** — And when Jehu was come to Jezreel, Jezebel heard of it; and she painted her face, and tired her head, and looked out at a window.... And he said, Throw her down. So they threw her down: and some of her blood was sprinkled on the wall, and on the horses: and he trode her under foot. And when he was come in, he did eat and drink, and said, Go, see now this cursed woman, and bury her: for she is a king's daughter. And they went to bury her: but they found no more of her than the skull, and the feet, and the palms of her hands. Wherefore they came again, and told him. And he said, This is the word of the Lord, which he spake by his servant Elijah the Tishbite, saying, In the portion of Jezreel shall dogs eat the flesh of Jezebel: And the carcase of Jezebel shall be as dung upon the face of the field in the portion of Jezreel; so that they shall not say, This is Jezebel.

5. **Proverbs 6:16-18** — These six things doth the Lord hate: yea, seven are an abomination unto him: a proud look, a lying tongue, and hands that shed innocent blood, an heart that deviseth wicked imaginations, feet that be swift in running to mischief, a false witness that speaketh lies, and he that soweth discord among brethren."

GREEK WORDS

1. "against" — κατὰ (*kata*): against; down; a strike against you

2. "because" — ὅτι (*hoti*): indicates expressly the reason

3. "sufferest" — ἀφίημι (*aphiemi*): to permit; to release; to let go; to liberate; to give unrestrained freedom

4. "that woman" — τὴν γυναῖκα (*ten gunaika*): with a definite article, the woman, indicating a woman of prominence; the two oldest manuscripts say "your wife," giving a strong impression that this Jezebel was the wife of the pastor in Thyatira

5. "a prophetess" — προφήτης (*prophetes*): a compound of the words πρό (*pro*) and φημί (*phemi*), meaning an interpreter or forth-teller of the divine will

6. "to seduce" — πλανάω (*planao*): deception; a moral wandering; depicts a person or nation that has veered from a solid path; as a result of veering morally, that person or nation is adrift; depicts a lost animal that cannot find its path; to morally lose one's bearings

7. "to commit fornication" — πορνεία (*porneia*): any type of sex with another person outside the bond of marriage; includes sexual activity by non-married individuals; includes both adultery and homosexuality

SYNOPSIS

As we have seen in previous lessons, Pergamum was a regal, royal city filled with vast treasures, exquisite architecture, and affluent people. To protect their wealth, the people of Pergamum established the city of Thyatira about 40 kilometers (25 miles) to the east. This military strong-hold was filled with thousands of soldiers and troops who were trained and equipped to defend Pergamum from any foreign invaders.

Thyatira was also home to a thriving church, which was birthed as a result of the preaching of the Gospel during the First Century. Jesus praised the believers there for their many good works, but He also corrected them for allowing a certain notable woman to seduce and corrupt the people. This "Jezebel," as He called her, was similar in character to the notorious Jezebel who was married to King Ahab in the Old Testament. Scholars believe that the Jezebel whom Jesus referred in the church of Thyatira was the pastor's wife.

The emphasis of this lesson:

Compromising God's standards displeases Him and is very costly. The lives of Ahab and Jezebel serve as examples of compromise that we want to avoid.

Jesus Spoke to the Pastor of the Church in Thyatira

We turn our attention once again to Revelation 2:18, where it says, "And unto the angel of the church in Thyatira write; These things saith the Son of God, who hath his eyes like unto a flame of fire, and his feet are like fine brass." We have seen that the word "angel" here is the Greek word *angelos*, which in this case doesn't refer to a heavenly being, but rather *an earthly messenger*. Specifically, it was *the pastor of the church* to whom Jesus was speaking, which is very important to understand in regard to this lesson.

Pastors are one of the fivefold ministry gifts that Christ has given His Church to establish us and bring unity and maturity to His Body. The responsibility of every pastor is to hear what the Lord is saying to the people he shepherds, to process it and apply it in his own life, and then to pass it on to the congregation. Whether the words of commendation or correction, the pastor is to share them faithfully in the anointing of the Holy Spirit. When Jesus addressed the "angel of the church in Thyatira," He was speaking to the pastor of that church.

The first words Jesus spoke were words of *praise*. He said, "I know thy works, and charity, and service, and faith, and thy patience, and thy works; and the last to be more than the first" (Revelation 2:19). Indeed, Thyatira had a great church that was doing great things. As we have seen in previous lessons, Jesus applauded the believers' unique expressions of love, their incredible acts of service, their sound biblical teaching, and their "never-give-up" endurance. They just kept getting better and better in these areas with each passing day. There was, however, something these believers were permitting that deeply disturbed Jesus.

They Had a Significant Strike Against Them

In Revelation 2:20, Jesus went on to say, "Notwithstanding I have a few things against thee, because thou sufferest that woman Jezebel, which calleth herself a prophetess, to teach and to seduce my servants to commit fornication, and to eat things sacrificed unto idols."

The word "notwithstanding" is the Greek word *alla*, which means *nonetheless*, *regardless*, or *in spite of all this*. This term denotes a marked shift or transition in the text — an interruption in the flow of thought. Thus, it could be translated, "In spite of all the wonderful things I just said about you, there is an issue I have against you."

This brings us to the phrase "I have" — the Greek word *echo*, which means *to have or hold something very closely*. The issue Jesus was about to address was something He felt very personally. "I have a few things against thee," He said. The word "against" is the Greek word *kata*, meaning *against*, *down*, or *a strike against you*. In spite of all the great works the believers at Thyatira had been doing, they had a major strike against their record, and it was one that Jesus held very close to His heart.

He said, "…Because thou sufferest that woman Jezebel, which calleth herself a prophetess, to teach and to seduce my servants to commit fornication, and to eat things sacrificed unto idols." The word "because" is the Greek word *hoti*, and it indicates *expressly the reason*. In essence, Jesus was saying, "I'm going to tell you exactly what the issue is that I have against you...." He then went on to describe the issue: "that thou sufferest that woman Jezebel."

The word "sufferest" is a form of the Greek word *aphiemi*, which means *to permit, to release; to let go; to liberate; to give unrestrained freedom*. The pastor of Thyatira had given free rein to "that woman Jezebel" to say and do whatever she pleased.

The phrase "that woman" means *the woman; the prominent woman; that woman of yours*; or *your wife*. It's important to note that the two oldest, most reliable manuscripts of the New Testament that are still in existence today translate this phrase "that woman of yours," which would be translated *"your wife Jezebel."* Remember, Jesus was speaking to the pastor of the church of Thyatira. That means Jezebel was likely the pastor's wife.

To clarify, not all pastors' wives are "Jezebels." In fact, most pastors' wives are heroes of the faith. They faithfully serve the Lord beside their husbands, sacrificing much and living selfless lives. The truth is, there are many wonderful things pastors' wives do behind the scenes that only God sees. Sadly, the wife of the pastor of Thyatira did not fall into this category.

A Doctrine of Compromise Was Corrupting the People

The Bible says that this Jezebel "calleth" herself a prophetess. The phrase "which calleth" in verse 20 is the Greek word *legousa*, and it means *that is alleging or asserting*. She was alleging to be "a prophetess," which we saw is the Greek word *prophetes*. It is a compound of the words *pro* and *phemi*, meaning *an interpreter or forth-teller of the divine will*. This woman was claiming to be something she was not.

Moreover, Jesus said that this woman Jezebel had been given unrestrained freedom "to teach and to seduce [His] servants to commit fornication." The words "to seduce" in the Greek is the word *planao*, and it describes *deception* or *a moral wandering*. It depicts *a person or nation who has veered morally from a solid path and, as a result, is adrift*. This is the same word used to *depict a lost animal that cannot find its way back to the path because it has wandered so far off track*.

The pastor's wife at the church of Thyatira, whom Jesus referred to as Jezebel, was using her husband's pulpit to lead the people in the wrong direction. Specifically, she was encouraging them to eat things sacrificed to idols and "to commit fornication." The phrase "to commit fornication" is from the Greek word *porneia*, which describes *any type of sex with another person outside the bond of marriage; it includes sexual activity by non-married individuals, including both adultery and homosexuality.*

If you remember from our previous lessons, the city of Thyatira had a highly developed system of trade guilds. Each guild had a patron pagan god, and at every gathering, guild members worshiped their god by offering sacrifices and participating in multiple forms of sexual immorality and drunkenness. Clearly, this was a place Christians didn't belong, but when they made a decision to refrain from these ungodly activities, their membership in the trade guild was revoked. Without work, Christians began to suffer financially.

Apparently, this woman called Jezebel was encouraging people to compromise their convictions, which was the same error being taught by the Nicolaitans at the churches in Ephesus and Pergamum (*see* Revelation 2:6,15). "It's okay to lower your standards," she asserted. "Don't terminate your membership in the trade guilds. Just blend in and participate a little so you can keep your job." But it was not okay with Jesus. It deeply disturbed Him, and He held these actions as a strike against the church of Thyatira.

What Do We Know About Jezebel From the Old Testament?

Although it is not likely that this prominent woman at the church of Thyatira was actually named Jezebel, she certainly acted like Jezebel from the Old Testament. According to First and Second Kings as well as historical documents, Jezebel was a foreigner to the land of Israel who came from the Phoenician city of Tyre. Her marriage to Ahab was a political arrangement to unify the people of Israel with the people of Phoenicia. Jezebel was a devout worshiper of Melkart, which was a form of Baal, the chief god of Phoenicia. When she came into Israel, she brought the worship of this god into the nation with her. In fact, she seems to have been a priestess and prophetess of Baal.

According to Second Kings 9:22 and 30, Jezebel was truly a wicked woman. She was actively involved in "whoredoms and witchcrafts," which are forms of the occult. She was idolatrous, cunning, manipulative, prideful, and disrespectful of spiritual authority. She even threatened the life of Elijah, the true prophet of God, claiming that her voice was equal to his (see 1 Kings 19:2). First Kings 18:4 says her wrath was so great against the genuine prophets of God that many of the prophets hid from her. The ones she could find, she killed. They were the voice of God, and she didn't want to hear what God had to say.

Jezebel supported those who adhered to her doctrines, placing hundreds and hundreds of prophets of Baal on the state payroll. With devious and deliberate manipulation, she controlled the people and the land of Israel indirectly through the throne that belonged to her husband, Ahab. First Kings 21:25 confirms this, stating, "But there was none like unto Ahab, which did sell himself to work wickedness in the sight of the Lord, whom Jezebel his wife stirred up." Day in and day out, this wicked queen incited her husband to do what was evil in the sight of God.

This is the character of Jezebel — one who controls from the outside. Thus, a "Jezebel" refers to any outside force — such as a spouse or a friend — who manipulates and controls. The wife of the pastor of the church in Thyatira fit this description.

Jezebel's Death Was Dreadful

In Second Kings 9:10, the end of Jezebel's life was prophesied. Through the prophet Elijah, God declared, "And the dogs shall eat Jezebel in the portion of Jezreel, and there shall be none to bury her...." By the time we come to verse 30, Ahab had been killed; Jehu had been anointed king in his place; and Jezebel was doing her best to remain in control of the kingdom of Israel through her son Joram.

The Bible says, "And when Jehu was come to Jezreel, Jezebel heard of it; and she painted her face, and tired her head, and looked out at a window" (2 Kings 9:30). At that point, Jezebel knew she was in trouble, but instead of humbling herself and submitting to the changes God had orchestrated, she defiantly painted her face and in pride looked down upon Jehu who was fast approaching.

The Bible says, "And he [Jehu] said, Throw her down. So they threw her down: and some of her blood was sprinkled on the wall, and on the horses: and he trode her under foot. And when he was come in, he did eat and drink, and said, Go, see now this cursed woman, and bury her: for she is a king's daughter. And they went to bury her: but they found no more of her than the skull, and the feet, and the palms of her hands" (2 Kings 9:33-37).

In an instant, the prophecy regarding Jezebel had been fulfilled. "Wherefore they came again, and told him [Jehu]. And he said, This is the word of the Lord, which he spake by his servant Elijah the Tishbite, saying, In the portion of Jezreel shall dogs eat the flesh of Jezebel: And the carcase of Jezebel shall be as dung upon the face of the field in the portion of Jezreel; so that they shall not say, This is Jezebel" (2 Kings 9:36,37).

Basically, Jezebel's body was devoured by dogs, and when the dogs were done, all that was left was their defecation to fertilize a nearby field — the same field Jezebel had stolen from a man named Naboth after she'd had him murdered. This brings up an interesting question: Why wouldn't the dogs eat Jezebel's feet, her skull, and the palms of her hands?

To answer this, we turn to Proverbs 6:16-19, which says, "These six things doth the Lord hate: yea, seven are an abomination unto him: a proud look, a lying tongue, and hands that shed innocent blood, an heart that deviseth wicked imaginations, feet that be swift in running to mischief, a false witness that speaketh lies, and he that soweth discord among brethren."

Jezebel had committed all seven of these abominations. In her mind, she was exceedingly proud and her thoughts were unclean. That is why the dogs didn't eat her skull. Likewise, the dogs didn't consume her hands because she had shed so much blood, and they wouldn't eat her feet because she was constantly running to mischief. The word of the Lord regarding the fate of this wicked woman had come to pass in every detail.

What Happened to Ahab?

Many people mistakenly believe that Ahab was a weak man, but history reveals that he was one of the strongest kings to ever rule Israel. During Ahab's reign, Israel was financially prosperous, and no one in the region was more politically powerful. Yet with all his power and influence, he didn't have the fortitude to deal with and control his wife. Ahab gave Jezebel free rein to do as she pleased.

This brings us back to the prominent woman in the church of Thyatira whom Jesus called "Jezebel." His message was to the pastor of the church, and the pastor's wife was the "Jezebel" to whom He was referring. In Jesus' great love, He was sending a sober warning to the pastor of Thyatira. The pastor was acting like Ahab — lacking the courage to control his wife and allowing her to do and say whatever she pleased. And because of the pastor's failure to stand in his God-given authority and put a stop to the evil his wife was perpetrating, this dangerous situation was about to derail the church of Thyatira.

Jesus warned the pastor, his wife "Jezebel," and the church members of their sin and called on them to repent. He gave them time to stop compromising and to turn their hearts and minds back into alignment with Him. And still today, Jesus gives people time to repent and return to Him.

If you have given place to a Jezebel or an Ahab spirit in your life, it's time to repent and make things right with God. If you will ask Him, He will give you the power to change.

STUDY QUESTIONS

Study to shew thyself approved unto God, a workman that needeth not to be ashamed, rightly dividing the word of truth.
— 2 Timothy 2:15

1. What new insights have you learned about Jezebel, Ahab, and the dangers of compromise?
2. Take a few moments to read and reflect on Proverbs 6:16-19. What is the Holy Spirit speaking to you through this passage?
3. Consider those in authority over your life — in your family, at work, and in government. In what ways can you better support and pray for them to stand firm and not give in to the temptation to compromise God's standards? (Consider 1 Timothy 2:1-4; Hebrews 13:17,18.)

PRACTICAL APPLICATION

But be ye doers of the word, and not hearers only, deceiving your own selves.
— James 1:22

The Bible says that manipulation is witchcraft in the eyes of the Lord. That is what a Jezebel spirit does — it attempts to manipulate and control things over which it has not been given authority. An Ahab spirit isn't any better. It shirks its responsibility and fails to bring correction to someone who is living in sin and/or is encouraging others to do so.

1. Be honest. Have you been acting like Jezebel? Have you possibly given place to the same wicked spirit that was operating through her? If you have, take time right now to repent and make things right with God. If you ask Him, He will give you the power to change.

2. Perhaps you have been acting more like Ahab — not standing and functioning in your God-given authority to stop attempts of the enemy to manipulate and exert wrong control through another person. If this describes you, pray and ask God to forgive you. If you ask Him, He will strengthen you to do what is right.

3. Be still and listen. What action steps do you sense the Holy Spirit is asking you to take at this time?

LESSON 6

TOPIC

What Does 'Space To Repent' Mean?

SCRIPTURES

1. **Revelation 2:18-21** — And unto the angel of the church in Thyatira write; These things saith the Son of God, who hath his eyes like unto a flame of fire, and his feet are like fine brass. I know thy works, and charity, and service, and faith, and thy patience, and thy works; and the last to be more than the first. Notwithstanding I have a few things against thee, because thou sufferest that woman Jezebel, which calleth herself a prophetess, to teach and to seduce my servants to commit fornication, and to eat things sacrificed unto idols. And I gave her space to repent of her fornication; and she repented not.

2. **1 Kings 21:25** — But there was none like unto Ahab, which did sell himself to work wickedness in the sight of the Lord, whom Jezebel his wife stirred up.

3. **1 Kings 18:21** — And Elijah came unto all the people, and said, How long halt ye between two opinions? if the LORD be God, follow him: but if Baal, then follow him. And the people answered him not a word.

4. **1 Kings 22:35,37,38** —blood ran out of the wound into the midst of the chariot. So the king died, and was brought to Samaria; and they

buried the king in Samaria. And one washed his chariot in the pool of Samaria; and the dogs licked up his blood....

GREEK WORDS

1. "notwithstanding" — ἀλλά (*alla*): nonetheless; regardless; but even in spite of this
2. "I have" — ἔχω (*echo*): to hold or to embrace; to hold something very personally
3. "against" — κατά (*kata*): against; down; a strike against you
4. "sufferest" — ἀφίημι (*aphiemi*): to permit, to release; to let go; to liberate; to give unrestrained freedom
5. "to seduce" — πλανάω (*planao*): deception; a moral wandering; depicts a person or nation that has veered from a solid path; as a result of veering morally, that person or nation is adrift; depicts a lost animal that cannot find its path; to morally lose one's bearings
6. "fornication" — πορνεία (*porneia*): any type of sex with another person outside the bond of marriage; includes sexual activity by non-married individuals; includes both adultery and homosexuality
7. "I gave" — ἔδωκα (*edoka*): I have given
8. "space" — χρόνος (*chronos*): time; a season; an epoch; an era; a specified duration of time
9. "repent" — μετανοήσῃ (*metanoese*): that she might repent; from μετανοέω (*metanoeo*), a change of mind that results in a complete, radical, total change of behavior; to completely change or to turn around in the way that one is thinking, believing, or living; a total transformation affecting every part of a person's life, both inside and outside, resulting in a behavioral change

SYNOPSIS

All that remains of the magnificent city of Thyatira today are hewn stones and fallen columns. Two thousand years ago, it was a thriving military outpost populated by thousands of Roman soldiers who were poised and positioned to quench the efforts of any eastern invaders to attack and plunder the city of Pergamum.

A powerful church had also been planted in Thyatira, and with each passing day, the believers there continued to make an eternal impact on the lives of those around them. Jesus praised them for their endeavors. He did, however, have one issue with the church — an issue that deeply disturbed Him. A notable woman He called "Jezebel" had been given free rein to teach error and lead people astray. Jesus despised her doctrine of compromise and told her to repent — or else she and the church would be judged.

The emphasis of this lesson:

Jesus gave the woman Jezebel time to repent and change her ways. Likewise, He gives us time to repent of our sinful ways. If we will hear and heed His words of warning, He will forgive us and restore us.

Jesus Was Faithful To Speak
to the Believers at Thyatira

In Revelation 2:18-29, Jesus spoke a message to the church of Thyatira, delivering it to the apostle John while John was imprisoned on the isle of Patmos. Jesus said, "And unto the angel of the church in Thyatira write; These things saith the Son of God, who hath his eyes like unto a flame of fire, and his feet are like fine brass. I know thy works, and charity, and service, and faith, and thy patience, and thy works; and the last to be more than the first" (vv. 18,19).

We have established that the word "angel" in verse 18 is the Greek word *angelos*. We saw that although it can describe a heavenly being, it is also used to describe *an earthly messenger*. In this passage, the word "angel" denotes *the pastor of the church in Thyatira*. As the God-appointed representative in the local church, this pastor's primary job was to hear the message the Lord is speaking, apply it personally to his own life, and then faithfully relay it to the congregation.

The first thing Jesus wanted the pastor of Thyatira to know and relay to the people is found in Revelation 2:19. He said, "I know thy works, and charity, and service, and faith, and thy patience, and thy works; and the last to be more than the first." Clearly, there were many great things Jesus had personally observed as He walked in the midst of this faithful congregation, and He was not negligent in voicing His commendation.

Jesus was also not slack in pointing out the sin to which the congregation in Thyatira had fallen prey. In Revelation 2:20, He said, "Notwithstanding

I have a few things against thee, because thou sufferest that woman Jezebel, which calleth herself a prophetess, to teach and to seduce my servants to commit fornication, and to eat things sacrificed unto idols." Let's briefly review the meaning behind the key words in this verse.

In Love, Jesus Corrects His Church

As we have noted, the word "notwithstanding" in Revelation 2:20 is the Greek word *alla*, which means *nonetheless, regardless*, or *even in spite of this*. It indicates a pause in the text where Jesus was transitioning from His words of commendation to His words of correction. It was the equivalent of Jesus saying, "In spite of all these wonderful things you are doing that I've just pointed out, there is an issue I must address." He then said, "I have a few things against thee...."

The words "I have" is a form of the Greek word *echo*, which means *to hold, to embrace*, or *to hold something very personally*. And the word "against" in Greek is the word *kata*, which describes *a downward strike against someone*. The issue Jesus was about to reveal to the pastor of the church in Thyatira was a strike against them that He held very close to His heart.

What was the issue? Jesus said, "...*Because* thou sufferest that woman Jezebel, which calleth herself a prophetess, to teach and to seduce my servants to commit fornication, and to eat things sacrificed unto idols" (Revelation 2:20). The word "because" is the Greek term *hoti*, and it indicates *explicit purpose*. By using this word, Jesus was saying, "I'm going to tell you exactly what you're doing that is grieving Me."

Notice Jesus' words: "...Thou sufferest that woman Jezebel...." The Greek word for "sufferest" is *aphiemi*, which means *to permit, to release, to let go, to liberate*, or *to give unrestrained freedom*. What was the pastor of the church in Thyatira permitting? To what was he giving unrestrained freedom? Jesus gave the answer: "that woman Jezebel" — which in the Greek says, *"the woman, the prominent woman, the notable woman in your church — Jezebel."* In the two earliest New Testament manuscripts that still exist, this phrase is translated, "that woman of yours." And because Jesus was saying, "that woman of yours" to the pastor of Thyatira, we can conclude reasonably that He was actually saying, "that *wife* of yours."

Apparently, the pastor of Thyatira had given his wife unrestrained freedom to do and say whatever she pleased, and her actions were leading many of the people astray. She was behaving just like the woman named Jezebel from the Old Testament — the woman who was married to the corrupt king named Ahab.

What Do We Know About Ahab?

Since the pastor's wife from the church of Thyatira was behaving like Jezebel, then it is likely the pastor was acting like Ahab. A Jezebel spirit can only operate where an Ahab spirit is in operation. An Ahab spirit liberates and empowers a Jezebel spirit to carry out its wicked ways.

Contrary to what many have believed, Ahab was *not* a weak man. History reveals that the army of Israel during his reign was extremely large and possibly the strongest it had ever been. Neighboring nations were terrified of Israel, and the rabbis of that time wrote that Ahab was the ruler of the world during his day.

Not only was Ahab a powerful military leader, but he also managed to bring the people of Israel into a very prosperous season — a time so plenteous that it was paralleled to the era of King Solomon. Indeed, Ahab's reign was marked by much peace and prosperity. He was able to control just about everything in his kingdom — everything except his wife Jezebel.

In an effort to establish peace and unity with the Phoenicians, Ahab had agreed to a politically arranged marriage with Jezebel. She was a Phoenician from the city of Tyre, the daughter of King Ethbaal of the Sidonians (*see* 1 Kings 16:31). When she came to Israel, she brought the worship of Baal with her. In an effort to appease his wife, Ahab erected a temple and an altar to Baal in the city of Samaria (*see* 1 Kings 16:32). Jezebel then placed hundreds of false prophets of Baal on the state payroll.

Clearly, God was not pleased with the actions of this husband-and-wife team. First Kings 21:25 says, "There was none like unto Ahab, which did sell himself to work wickedness in the sight of the Lord, whom Jezebel his wife stirred up." Jezebel manipulated Ahab like a puppet in her hand, causing him to vacillate in his faith. Consequently, the entire nation of Israel, like Ahab, wobbled between devotion to God and the worship of Baal.

First Kings 18:21 says, "Elijah came unto all the people, and said, How long halt ye between two opinions? if the Lord be God, follow him: but if Baal, then follow him. And the people answered him not a word." The

Israelites couldn't answer Elijah and make a decision regarding whom they would serve because of the indecision in the heart of their covering — King Ahab. What was on the head of the nation had come upon the body of the nation.

The Point of No Return for Ahab and Jezebel

In the course of time, Ahab sought to purchase the vineyard of a man named Naboth who lived next door to his palace. He offered Naboth the choice of another piece of land or money in exchange for his vineyard, but Naboth rejected the offer. Discouraged and depressed, Ahab returned home and lay on his bed, refusing to eat (*see* 1 Kings 21:1-4).

When Jezebel saw Ahab sulking and saddened and had learned what had happened, she immediately went to work concocting a scheme to secure the land. Writing letters in Ahab's name, she manipulated two people into falsely accusing Naboth of blaspheming God and the king. For Naboth's alleged crime, Jezebel ordered that he be stoned to death. Once the murderous deed had been done, she told Ahab of Naboth's death and instructed him to go and take possession of the land (*see* 1 Kings 21:5-15).

Ahab knew the property had been wrongfully attained, but he took possession of it anyway. This was exceedingly offensive in God's eyes, and He held Ahab responsible for Naboth's death because he wouldn't control Jezebel's activities. Immediately God sent Elijah the prophet to speak judgment on Ahab. The Lord told Elijah, "And thou shalt speak unto him, saying, Thus saith the Lord, Hast thou killed, and also taken possession? …In the place where the dogs licked the blood of Naboth shall the dogs lick thy blood, even thine" (1 Kings 21:19).

Approximately three years later, King Ahab was mortally wounded in battle, "…and the blood ran out of the wound into the midst of the chariot. So the king died, and was brought to Samaria; and they buried the king in Samaria. And one washed the chariot in the pool of Samaria; and the dogs licked up his blood…" (1 Kings 22:35,37,38). The Septuagint, which is the Greek translation of the Old Testament, says that *dogs* and *pigs* licked up Ahab's blood. To the people of Israel, pigs were unclean. The fact that pigs would lick up his blood signifies the extent to which Ahab had sold himself to uncleanness.

This act was the point of no return for Ahab and for Jezebel. Not only would her blood be licked up by dogs, but her body would be consumed by them. This was prophesied by Elijah, and it came to pass shortly thereafter when Jehu, the newly anointed king of Israel, came riding into town to carry out the Lord's work (*see* 2 Kings 9:30-37).

Jezebel and Ahab of the Old Testament vs. the 'Jezebel and Ahab' of the Church in Thyatira

Evidently, the pastor of the church in Thyatira was behaving similarly to Ahab of the Old Testament. He was vacillating between two positions: believing and acting on the truth of God's Word — but permitting the doctrine of compromise his wife Jezebel was propagating. This New Testament "Ahab" had shirked his responsibility as the head of his home and the shepherd of his church. Consequently, Jesus brought correction to him and to the woman He called Jezebel.

In Revelation 2:21, Jesus declared, "I gave her space to repent of her fornication; and she repented not." Notice the phrase "I gave." It is the Greek word *edoka*, which means *I have given*. And the word "space" is the Greek word *chronos*, which describes *time; a season, an epoch, an era*, or *a specified duration of time*. The combined use of these words tells us that Jesus had already personally given Jezebel a specified amount of time to make things right.

He had told her to "repent" — taken from the word *metanoeo*, which describes *a change of mind that results in a complete, radical, total change of behavior; to completely change or to turn around in the way that one is thinking, believing, or living; or a total transformation affecting every part of a person's life, both inside and outside, resulting in a behavioral change.*

For what did Jesus give this Jezebel time to repent? The Bible says "fornication," which is the Greek word *porneia*. It describes *any type of sex with another person outside the bond of marriage*. It refers to *sexual activity by non-married individuals, including both adultery and homosexuality.*

Was the Jezebel in Thyatira — who we understand was most likely the pastor's wife — committing fornication? We do not know. What we do know is that in order for the believers in Thyatira to continue as members of their perspective trade guilds and keep their jobs, they needed to compromise God's standards and participate in idol worship, drunkenness, and fornication. It seems this prominent woman was using her husband's position of influence to seduce God's servants into compromise, saying things like, "It's okay to lower your standards and participate in the activities. Go ahead and blend in with everyone else. God understands your situation." It was for this behavior that Jesus gave Jezebel time to repent — but we discover from Jesus' words that she repented not.

STUDY QUESTIONS

Study to shew thyself approved unto God, a workman that needeth not to be ashamed, rightly dividing the word of truth.
— 2 Timothy 2:15

God corrects us because He loves us, and at times every one of us requires His correction. We all have times when we drift off course and need His discipline in our lives. Even King David — a man after God's own heart — needed correction. Take a few moments to reflect on David's response to God in Psalm 32:1-6 after he repented of his sin with Bathsheba.

1.   What happens when you choose *not* to repent and to "come clean" with God?

2.   What takes place when you do repent and ask God to forgive you of sin?

3.   According to verse 6, why is it urgent that you take the opportunity to repent when the Lord reveals sin in your heart? (*See* also 2 Corinthians 6:1,2; Hebrews 3:7-9,15; 4:7.)

4.   What is the Holy Spirit showing you in this passage?

PRACTICAL APPLICATION

But be ye doers of the word, and not hearers only, deceiving your own selves.
—James 1:22

1.   Have you ever had a time in your life when you waited too long to repent? If so, briefly describe what happened.

2.   What kind of symptoms did you experience? How did your slowness to repent impact your relationship with God? How did it affect your relationship with others?

3.   What did God use to finally get your attention and soften your heart to repent?

TOPIC

What Is Repentance?

SCRIPTURES

1. **Revelation 2:18-22** — And unto the angel of the church in Thyatira write; These things saith the Son of God, who hath his eyes like unto a flame of fire, and his feet are like fine brass. I know thy works, and charity, and service, and faith, and thy patience, and thy works; and the last to be more than the first. Notwithstanding I have a few things against thee, because thou sufferest that woman Jezebel, which calleth herself a prophetess, to teach and to seduce my servants to commit fornication, and to eat things sacrificed unto idols. And I gave her space to repent of her fornication; and she repented not. Behold, I will cast her into a bed, and them that commit adultery with her into great tribulation, except they repent of their deeds.

2. **1 Samuel 2:17** — Wherefore, the sin of the young men was very great before the Lord…

GREEK WORDS

1. "I gave" — **ἔδωκα** (*edoka*): I have given

2. "space" — **χρόνος** (*chronos*): time; a season; an epoch; an era; a specified duration of time

3. "repent" — **μετανοήσῃ** (*metanoese*): that she might repent; from **μετανοέω** (*metanoeo*), a change of mind that results in a complete, radical, total change of behavior; to completely change or to turn around in the way that one is thinking, believing, or living; a total transformation affecting every part of a person's life, both inside and outside, resulting in a behavioral change

4. "Behold" — **ἰδού** (*idou*): bewilderment; shock; amazement; wonder

5. "into a bed" — **εἰς κλίνην** (*eis kleinen*): a bed; a funeral bier

6. "tribulation" — **θλῖψις** (*thlipsis*): great pressure; crushing pressures

7. "except" — **ἐὰν** (*ean*): shows that the warning is conditional; it may or may not happen depending on how the hearer responds; if conditions are met to change, the warning will be voided

8. "deeds" — ἔργων (*ergon*): deeds, actions, or activities

SYNOPSIS

Thyatira was a powerful city located in the Roman province of Asia — the area known today as Turkey. During the First Century, the streets of this city were teeming with thousands of Roman soldiers. They had been stationed to protect and defend the rich and resplendent neighboring city of Pergamum, which was situated about 40 kilometers (25 miles) to the west.

In the First Century, Thyatira was a very dark place entrenched in sexual debauchery, drunkenness, demonic activity, and pagan practices. Nevertheless, preachers came and presented the message of the Gospel, and the Gospel did what only the Gospel can do — driving back the powers of darkness and allowing the Church of the Lord Jesus to be established in the city.

Although the church of Thyatira was doing many great works, it was also permitting a woman called "Jezebel" to teach and seduce God's servants to commit fornication. For this reason, Jesus called the church, its pastor, and the woman Jezebel to repent.

Although there is much confusion over the topic of repentance in the Church today, Jesus is still calling us to repent. Just as He was patient and merciful and gave Jezebel space to repent, He gives us space to repent too.

The emphasis of this lesson:

There is no expiration date on the practice of repentance. It was for the Church at the beginning, and it is still for the Church today. Repentance is a decision that results in a total transformation affecting every part of a person's life.

Jesus Commended and Corrected the Church of Thyatira

In Revelation 2:18 and 19, Jesus spoke to the pastor of the church in Thyatira, saying, "These things saith the Son of God, who hath his eyes like unto a flame of fire, and his feet are like fine brass. I know thy works, and charity, and service, and faith, and thy patience, and thy works; and the last to be more than the first." Up to this point, everything Christ had said about the believers in Thyatira was wonderful. This was a church of genuine love, excellence in ministry, steadfast endurance, and sound scriptural teaching.

Then in verse 20, Jesus shifted His attention to an area where the church was coming up short. He said, "Notwithstanding I have a few things against thee, because thou sufferest that woman Jezebel, which calleth herself a prophetess, to teach and to seduce my servants to commit fornication, and to eat things sacrificed unto idols."

We have learned that the word "notwithstanding" in Greek is the word *alla*, which means *nonetheless* or *in spite of*, and the phrase "I have" is a form of the Greek word *echo*, which means *to hold or to embrace* or *to hold something very personally*. Moreover, the word "against" is the Greek word *kata*, which describes *a downward strike against someone*. Taking these three words into account, the beginning of verse 20 was the equivalent of Jesus saying, "In spite of all the wonderful things I've just said about you, there is a strike against you that I personally hold very deeply and consider quite disturbing."

Jezebel Was Promoting a Doctrine of Compromise

What was the pastor of Thyatira doing that evoked Jesus' rebuke? The pastor was giving the notable woman Jesus referred to as "Jezebel" unrestrained freedom to say and do whatever she pleased. The two earliest New Testament manuscripts we have actually say "that woman of yours," which indicates that Jezebel was most likely the pastor's wife. What's more, she was calling herself a "prophetess," which is the Greek word *prophetes*, and it describes *one who claims to have divine revelation and speaks on behalf of God*. In reality, she didn't have any new revelation from God. She had only a modification of the truth, and she was teaching it to God's servants and was leading them astray.

To be clear, the Bible is not saying that women shouldn't teach. The problem with this woman whom Jesus called Jezebel was *not* that she was teaching. The problem was *what* she was teaching. She was *teaching error* and *abusing her husband's position of authority* by leading people into compromise that lead them into sin. The phrase "to seduce" is the Greek word *planao*, which means *to wander aimlessly* or *to lead others off track morally*. This woman was causing people to veer from the solid path of Scripture they had once held so tightly.

In Thyatira, there was a highly developed system of trade guilds that dominated the employment landscape. Each guild had its own patron god that was worshiped at each meeting. Guild members were required to bow in worship to idols, to offer sacrifices to idols, and to eat the foods that had been sacrificed to idols. Drunkenness, orgies, and fornication of all kinds were a regular part of the trade-guild life. Christians who refused to participate in these activities had their membership revoked and were blacklisted from receiving employment. Those who were not a part of a trade guild were without a job, which caused financial struggles for many believers.

Apparently, the "Jezebel" in Thyatira was teaching a doctrine of compromise. She must have been saying things like, "Go ahead and attend the trade-guild meetings so you can keep your jobs and avoid being blacklisted. Lower your standards a little, and learn to blend in with the people you work with. It's okay to respectfully bow to the patron god of your guild and eat the food sacrificed to it. You're not going to lose your salvation."

It seems this was the message that this Jezebel was packaging and promoting, and it was seducing Jesus' servants into committing fornication. She was teaching a doctrine of compromise, just as the Nicolaitans were teaching in the church of Ephesus (*see* Revelation 2:6) and the church of Pergamum (*see* Revelation 2:15).

Christ hates compromise because He knows where it leads. When His people fall into compromise, it pulls the plug on the power of the Holy Spirit manifesting in their midst. Indeed, compromise is fatal to the life of His Church.

Jesus Gives Us Time To Repent

Once Jesus clearly revealed the issue He held personally against the church of Thyatira, He then said, "And I gave her [Jezebel] space to repent of her fornication; and she repented not" (Revelation 2:21). The phrase "I gave" is the Greek word *edoka*, which means *I have personally given — past tense.* Jesus loved this woman and was personally involved in helping her work out her salvation.

He gave her "space" to repent. The word "space" is the Greek word *chronos*, which means *time; a season, a specified duration of time.* Sadly, the Bible says she repented not. Interestingly, in the three oldest manuscripts, the phrase "she repented not" reads as, "she willeth not to repent out of her fornication." In other words, when she heard the Lord's correction and call to repentance, she deliberately rejected His request and willfully chose not to cooperate. She defiantly disobeyed Him and kept on doing the very things He had personally asked her to stop doing.

A great example from Scripture of God giving someone *space* to repent and change is the story of Eli the high priest and his two sons, Hophni and Phineas. This entire family was in ministry, but Hophni and Phineas were wicked and had no regard for the Lord (*see* 1 Samuel 2:12). In fact, they had veered off track so seriously that they were even stealing from the people's offerings and fornicating with women who worked in the temple (*see* 1 Samuel 2:14,22).

Exactly how long this situation was tolerated, we don't know. However, it seems to have persisted over a lengthy period of time. Eli knew what his two sons were doing — yet he did not restrain them or remove them from their positions.

This is exactly what the pastor of the church in Thyatira did. He was fully aware of what his wife was doing, yet he wouldn't restrain her.

Judgment for Hophni and Phineas' behavior did *not* come quickly. Like Jezebel in Thyatira, God gave them *space* to repent. His action against these priests was not released until they had ample time to turn from their wicked ways and to change.

A careful look at history shows that God is extremely patient and even "tolerates" sin for a period of time. Nevertheless, First Samuel 2:17 makes it clear that God does not overlook the greatness of a person's sin. Although He is merciful, there comes a moment in time when the clock runs out and even in His mercy, judgment must ensue.

Eventually Eli and his sons were judged — and when judgment came, it occurred quickly. Once it was clear that their behavior was not going to change and that Eli was not going to exercise his authority to stop it, God released His judgment, and Eli and his sons were removed in a single day (*see* 1 Samuel 4:11-18).

What Does It Mean To Repent?

This brings us to the word "repent," which is used by Jesus three times in Revelation 2:21,22. "Repent" is from the Greek word *metanoeo*, and it means *a change of mind that results in a complete, radical, total change of behavior; to completely change or to turn around in the way that one is thinking, believing, or living;* or *a total transformation affecting every part of a person's life, both inside and outside, resulting in a behavioral change.*

Make no mistake. Real repentance produces behavioral change, both inward and outward. When God tells us to repent, He wants to see change in our conduct, not an emotional response. Repentance isn't crying, grieving, or even regretting. It is a decision of the will to change. Jesus said He had personally given Jezebel a specified amount of time to repent, but she had rejected the divine offer of mercy and instead continued down the path of rebellion that would ultimately lead to judgment.

Friend, if God is correcting you and calling you to repent in any area of your life, then you must make the decision to do so. Line up your will with His and cooperate with the Holy Spirit and do what He says to do. He will join His power to you when you make the decision to change, and it will enable you to change the way you are thinking, believing, and living.

Even With Judgment Looming, Jesus Extends Mercy

After Jezebel willfully chose not to repent, Jesus said, "Behold, I will cast her into a bed, and them that commit adultery with her into great tribulation, except they repent of their deeds" (Revelation 2:22). Notice the word "Behold." It is the Greek word *idou*, which describes *bewilderment, shock, amazement,* or *wonder.* When Jesus said, "Behold," it was as if He was saying, "Wow! What I'm about to say to you is so amazing, it leaves Me virtually speechless."

He then announced the punishment that was looming: "I will cast her into a bed...." The phrase "into a bed" in Greek is *eis kleinen*, which describes *a bed* or *a funeral bier.* In other words, Jesus was saying, "I'm going to place this woman in a casket and bury her for her refusal to repent for what she's done."

And to Jezebel's accomplices, Jesus said, "...and them that commit adultery with her into great tribulation...." The word "tribulation" is the Greek word *thlipsis*, which describes *great pressure* or *crushing pressures.* Here we see a differentiation in the way the Lord deals with people. The greater punishment was assigned to Jezebel for initiating and propagating the error. Nonetheless, those who believed her lies — and those could have stopped her from teaching those lies but didn't — would experience a period of difficulty as Jesus dealt with them.

Then Jesus added, "…except they repent of their deeds." Even after all these people had done, He was still hopeful that Jezebel and her co-conspirators would repent. The word "except" — the Greek word *ean* — shows that the warning is *conditional*. In other words, *the consequences may or may not happen, depending on how the hearer responds*. In this case, if the conditions were met and the parties involved changed, Jesus' warning would be voided.

It is important to note that the word "deeds" is the Greek word *ergon*, which describes *deeds*, *actions*, or *activities*. By using this word, it lets us know that Jesus didn't just want Jezebel and her cohorts to say they were sorry; He wanted them to "repent of their deeds." He was after complete behavioral change, both inside and out. He wanted them to adjust not only their actions and activities, but the way they thought and believed.

This is the same thing God is after in you when He reveals an issue of sin in your life. He wants you to choose to make a 180-degree turn in that area — a radical change from the inside out — and then to adjust your actions to reflect your decision.

STUDY QUESTIONS

Study to shew thyself approved unto God, a workman that needeth not to be ashamed, rightly dividing the word of truth.
— 2 Timothy 2:15

Although it may seem like God is ignoring people's sin and wickedness, He is actually extending mercy and patiently giving them space to repent. If you find yourself frustrated and angry as you watch the wicked seemingly getting away with sinful and unjust ways, check out Psalm 37.

1. What does God want you to always keep in mind about the end of those who do evil? (*See* verses 1,2,9,10,14,15,20,35,36.)

2. While the wicked are busy following their own lawless agenda, how does God expect you to live? (*See* verses 3-7,27,34.)

3. As you choose to obey God and live right, what blessings does He promise to give you? (*See* verses 6,11,17-19,22-29,37-40.)

PRACTICAL APPLICATION

But be ye doers of the word, and not hearers only,
deceiving your own selves.
— James 1:22

1. Prior to this lesson, what was your perspective of *repentance*? How has your understanding of this vital subject changed? What is the Holy Spirit speaking to you personally about repentance?

2. It is vital to understand the unique differences between *worldly sorrow* and *godly sorrow*. Take a few moments to read Second Corinthians 7:9-11 and identify the characteristics produced by each. How does this understanding give you a better appreciation for the conviction of sin the Holy Spirit brings to you?

LESSON 8

TOPIC

What Causes God To Judge Someone Today?

SCRIPTURES

1. **Revelation 2:18-23** — And unto the angel of the church in Thyatira write; These things saith the Son of God, who hath his eyes like unto a flame of fire, and his feet are like fine brass. I know thy works, and charity, and service, and faith, and thy patience, and thy works; and the last to be more than the first. Notwithstanding I have a few things against thee, because thou sufferest that woman Jezebel, which calleth herself a prophetess, to teach and to seduce my servants to commit fornication, and to eat things sacrificed unto idols. And I gave her space to repent of her fornication; and she repented not. Behold, I will cast her into a bed, and them that commit adultery with her into great tribulation, except they repent of their deeds. And I will kill her children with death; and all the churches shall know that I am he which searcheth the reins and hearts: and I will give unto every one of you according to your works.

2. **1 Corinthians 3:16,17** — Know ye not that ye are the temple of God, and that the Spirit of God dwelleth in you? If any man defile the temple of God, him shall God destroy; for the temple of God is holy, which temple ye are.

GREEK WORDS

1. "Behold" — **ἰδού** (*idou*): bewilderment; shock; amazement; wonder
2. "into a bed" — **εἰς κλίνην** (*eis kleinen*): a bed; a funeral bier
3. "tribulation" — **θλῖψις** (*thlipsis*): great pressure; crushing pressures
4. "except" — **ἐὰν** (*ean*): shows that the warning is conditional; it may or may not happen depending on how the hearer responds; if conditions are met to change, the warning will be voided
5. "deeds" — **ἔργων** (*ergon*): deeds; actions; activities
6. "repent" — **μετανοήσῃ** (*metanoese*): that she might repent; from **μετανοέω** (*metanoeo*), a change of mind that results in a complete, radical, total change of behavior; to completely change or to turn around in the way that one is thinking, believing, or living; a total transformation affecting every part of a person's life, both inside and outside, resulting in a behavioral change
7. "I will kill" — **ἀποκτείνω** (*apokteino*): to slaughter; to put an abrupt end to; can denote the giving of a death sentence
8. "children" — **τέκνα** (*tekna*): children; offspring
9. "death" — **θάνατος** (*thanatos*): pictures finality; mortal danger or a dangerous circumstance
10. "shall know" — **γινώσκω** (*ginosko*): to know; to perceive; to comprehend
11. "searches" — **ἐρευνάω** (*ereunao*): to search; to work through all the materials and evidence to obtain a full picture; an investigation that yields correct conclusions
12. "reins" — **νεφρός** (*nephros*): kidneys; in the New Testament, denotes the human spirit; the depths of a person's being
13. "hearts" — **καρδία** (*kardia*): the heart; depicts emotion and passion
14. "I will give" — **δώσω** (*doso*): the future; personal form of **δίδωμι**; I will personally give; I will personally bestow; I will personally deliver
15. "every man" — **ἔκαστος** (*hekastos*): an all-inclusive term that embraces everyone, no one excluded

16. "according" — **κατά** (*kata*): exactly according to; indicates a full accounting of the facts
17. "works" — **ἔργα** (*erga*): deeds; actions; activities
18. "defile" and "destroy" — **φθείρω** (*phtheiro*): to spoil, plunder, destroy, empty, or wipe out

SYNOPSIS

The city of Thyatira was a military outpost whose primary reason for existence was to protect and defend the wealthy city of Pergamum from eastern invaders. It was a dark and treacherous place, filled with demonic activity and pagan practices. Yet into this wicked region, the Gospel entered and penetrated the darkness, pushing back the powers of evil and establishing the church of Thyatira.

This church was having an amazing impact on the community, and Jesus praised them for their efforts. Unfortunately, as time passed, they had begun to tolerate and give place to a doctrine of compromise that was being taught by a prominent woman in leadership. Jesus was personally aware of the situation and gave them a space of time to repent and come back into alignment with truth. If they would not repent of their deeds and self-correct their course, Jesus would bring the judgment He had warned them about.

The emphasis of this lesson:

God is merciful and doesn't wish to bring judgment on anyone. Yet if someone willfully rejects His space of time to repent and change their ways, His judgment will come.

Revelation 2:18-20 says, "And unto the angel of the church in Thyatira write; These things saith the Son of God, who hath his eyes like unto a flame of fire, and his feet are like fine brass. I know thy works, and charity, and service, and faith, and thy patience, and thy works; and the last to be more than the first. Notwithstanding I have a few things against thee, because thou sufferest that woman Jezebel, which calleth herself a prophetess, to teach and to seduce my servants to commit fornication, and to eat things sacrificed unto idols."

It is important to point out that these are the words of Jesus Himself. John was the one who wrote them, but they came straight from the mouth of Christ. There was a notable woman in Thyatira whom Jesus likened unto Jezebel of the Old Testament. This woman was using her position of influence to coax people into believing it was okay to lower their Christian standards and blend in with the world. Like the Nicolaitans had done in the churches of Pergamum and Ephesus, this Jezebel was teaching a doctrine of compromise, and it was about to bring the judgment of God upon them.

Jezebel Seduced God's Servants To Lower Their Standards

The Bible states that this Jezebel in the church of Thyatira had been given unrestrained freedom "to teach and to seduce" Christ's servants into committing fornication. The words "to seduce" is the Greek word *planao*, which means *to cause one to wander morally off the proven path of truth*. It is not likely that this woman was blatantly saying, "Hey, let's all go and commit adultery and eat the foods sacrificed to idols." But she *was* encouraging believers to blend in with the people of the world, even if it meant participating in their pagan activities.

As we have noted, the city of Thyatira was governed by a system of trade guilds. In order for a person to secure steady work, he had to become a member of a trade guild. These labor unions operated on a buddy system in which new jobs were passed on to fellow members. Anyone who chose to no longer attend guild meetings and participate in guild activities had his membership revoked and was blacklisted, which meant he couldn't get another job.

Christians in Thyatira didn't want to go to trade-guild meetings because of the sinful practices that were going on there. At every meeting, members were required to bow before the patron pagan god of their guild and then burn incense and offer sacrifices to that god. Drunkenness, fornication, and feasting on the meat sacrificed to idols were integral parts of each gathering. It was a godless, demonic environment that believers didn't need to participate in.

Emboldened by the Spirit, Christians in Thyatira had taken a stand for righteousness. They had said, "We are the Church — the *ekklesia* or called-out ones. God has called us out of darkness, and we're not going back into that wicked environment even if it means losing our jobs."

The woman Jezebel — who most likely was the pastor's wife, according to the wording in the earliest New Testament manuscripts — began advising God's servants to compromise. Apparently her message to the people was to do whatever they needed to do to keep their jobs and maintain a steady income. The Scripture says she called herself a prophetess and claimed to speak with God's voice. Through her position of influence, this Jezebel effectively began seducing believers back into environments that were spiritually detrimental. This was a major strike against this church and its pastor, who had not restrained her in any way, and Jesus held the infraction very close to His heart.

Jesus Personally Appealed to Jezebel to Repent

In Revelation 2:21, Jesus said, "And I gave her space to repent of her fornication; and she repented not." The words "I gave" in Greek indicates that Jesus had already given — *past tense* — this woman Jezebel "space," which means *time or a season*, to repent. He had been personally involved in her life, encouraging her to repent so that she could be restored and avoid experiencing His judgment.

As we learned previously, the word "repent" is from the Greek word *metanoeo*, and it describes *a change of mind that results in a complete, radical, total change of behavior, a total transformation affecting every part of a person's life, both inside and outside, resulting in a behavioral change.* Jesus gave Jezebel a season of time to repent, and He also gives us time to repent. He doesn't want to bring judgment on anyone. He took the judgment for our sins upon Himself when He was crucified on the Cross. When we disobey Him, all we need to do is sincerely repent. This means asking Jesus to forgive us and change us and then choosing to turn away from wrong behavior.

When someone in the Church — such as this woman Jezebel — refuses to repent, Jesus has no other choice but to deal with the person. Sin that is left unchecked is like an infectious disease that can rapidly spread throughout the Body.

When a person has cancer, physicians seek to eradicate it from a person's body. When someone in the Body of Christ is living in unrepentant sin — especially someone with influence — Jesus, the Great Physician, will move to eradicate that person's influence from *His* Body.

Jesus said, "I gave her space to repent of her fornication; and she repented not" (Revelation 2:21). As we noted in the last lesson, the earliest New Testament manuscripts say, "She willed not to repent out of her fornication." This woman Jesus called Jezebel heard His voice beckoning to her to repent, and she knew that what she was teaching was wrong and leading believers astray. Yet she deliberately chose not to repent and correct her ways. Thus, Jesus had no other choice but to respond to her rebellion.

The Judgment for Wrongdoing Was Clear

In Revelation 2:22, Jesus said, "Behold, I will cast her into a bed...." The word "behold" is the Greek word *idou*, and it describes *bewilderment*, *shock*, *amazement*, and *wonder*. The use of this word indicates that what Jesus was about to say was so astounding and so amazing, He was virtually speechless.

The phrase "I will cast" comes from the Greek word *ballo*, which means *to throw* or *to hurl*. The tense here indicates immediacy. In other words, Jesus was saying, "Right now, at this very moment, I'm going to deal with her [Jezebel] by hurling her into a bed." The phrase "into a bed" in Greek is *eis kleinen*, which can be translated as *a bed* or *a couch*. It is usually used to describe *a sickbed*. It's interesting to note that the word for "bed" can also be translated as *a funeral bier*. By using this word, Jesus was basically saying, "I'm going to put an end to this woman's activities. I'm going to put her, her doctrines, and her deeds out of commission."

Jesus went on to say, "....and them that commit adultery with her into great tribulation...." Since Jezebel was the source and instigator behind the false teaching, she would be dealt with more severely. Those "that commit adultery with her" were the people who believed in, acted on, and encouraged what she said. It also included those who were silent about what she was doing and chose not to place any restraint on her. Whatever the case, these co-conspirators were going to experience "great tribulation" for the role they played.

The word "tribulation" in Greek is *thlipsis*, and it describes *great pressure* or *crushing pressures*. When you enter into the arena of sin, you are putting yourself in a place of great pressure. These believers who were in league with the Jezebel of Thyatira had placed themselves in a very bad position. Jesus knew this hence, He continued to warn them to repent.

After pinpointing the pending judgment, Jesus extended mercy yet again by saying, "…except they repent of their deeds." The word "except" is the Greek word *ean*, and it shows that the warning is *conditional*. In other words, *it may or may not happen, depending on how the hearer responds*. If conditions are met and the required change is implemented, the judgment Jesus warned of would be voided. He was calling on everyone involved to repent of their "deeds"— the Greek word *ergon*, which describes *deeds*, *actions*, or *activities*. He didn't just want a verbal "I'm sorry." He wanted those whose actions had qualified them for this warning to make the decision to change their behavior.

Before Jesus Takes Action, He Thoroughly Investigates

In Revelation 2:23, Jesus said something that is very difficult for most believers hear. Continuing His words of correction to the church of Thyatira, He vowed, "And I will kill her children with death; and all the churches shall know that I am he which searcheth the reins and hearts: and I will give unto every one of you according to your works."

First, notice the phrase "I will kill." In Greek, it is the word *apokteino*, which means *to slaughter* or *to put an abrupt end to*. It can also denote *the giving of a death sentence*. What was it that Jesus said He was going to put an abrupt end to? Verse 23 says "her children." In Greek, the word "children" is *tekna*, and it signifies *children or offspring*. Essentially Jesus was saying, "I'm going to slaughter, eliminate, and put out of commission the fruit born from her teaching." How was He going to do it? This scripture gives the answer: "with death." The word "death" here is the Greek word *thanatos*, which pictures *finality*, *mortal danger*, or *a dangerous circumstance*.

Jesus went on to say, "…All the churches shall know that I am he which searcheth the reins and hearts…" (Revelation 2:23). The phrase "shall know" is the future tense of the Greek word *ginosko*, which means *to know*, *to perceive*, or *to comprehend*. By using this word, Jesus was saying, "All the churches shall understand and truly comprehend what I think of the doctrine of compromise." When judgment comes to the house of God, it sends a clear message to the entire Body. Believers everywhere understand things about Him that they have never before comprehended.

The word "searcheth" in verse 23 is also significant. It comes from the Greek word *ereunao*, which means *to search; to work through all the materials and evidence to obtain a full picture;* or *an investigation that yields correct conclusions.* This word lets us know the meticulousness in which Jesus operates. He takes no action until He thoroughly investigates and sees the full picture.

What does Jesus thoroughly search? He said "the *reins* and *hearts.*" The word "reins" in this verse is the Greek word *nephros,* which means *kidneys.* In the New Testament, it denotes *the human spirit* or *the depths of a person's being.* The word "hearts" in Greek is *kardia.* In addition to describing *the human heart,* it depicts *emotion and passion.* When the Bible says Jesus "searcheth the reins and hearts," it means He thoroughly investigates a person's soul and spirit, carefully examining emotions, instincts, and passions. Every part is examined from every angle until all is brought to light.

Once a full investigation is concluded, Jesus explained what came next: "…I will give unto every one of you according to your works." In Greek, the phrase "I will give" is the word *doso,* and it describes *a very personal involvement in the act of giving* on the part of Jesus. Essentially, He was saying, "I will personally give; I will personally bestow; and I will personally deliver." And this very personal act is to "every one of you," which is a phrase from the Greek word *hekastos.* It is *an all-inclusive term that embraces everyone, no one excluded.*

As a child of God, you have a promise from Jesus Himself to personally give and deliver to you "according to your works." The word "according" in Greek is the word *kata,* which in this case means *exactly according to.* It indicates *a full accounting of the facts.*

After Jesus has fully investigated, He is going to give us exactly what we deserve according to our "works." This word "works" is again the Greek word *erga,* which describes *deeds, actions,* or *activities.*

Does Jesus Still Judge People Today?

Some people wonder, *If Christ received God's judgment on the Cross for our sin and the sin of the world, does God still judge people today?* This is a good question, and you need to know the answer. First, God does not judge us for past sin that we have already repented of. Those past sins are under the blood and removed from us as far as the east is from the west (*see* Psalm 103:12).

However, the Bible makes it clear that God will judge any leader or believer who wrongfully handles the Church. If we "defile" or "destroy" God's temple, we put ourselves in danger. First Corinthians 3:16 and 17 says, "Know ye not that ye are the temple of God, and that the Spirit of God dwelleth in you? If any man defile the temple of God, him shall God destroy; for the temple of God is holy, which temple ye are."

You are the "temple" of God, and that word "temple" is the Greek word *naos*, which describes *a highly decorated shrine*. As a believer, you are the highly decorated habitation, or house, of the Spirit of God on the earth. You are a part of His Church, and the Church is precious in God's sight — so much so that He says, "…If any man defile the temple of God, him shall God destroy…" (1 Corinthians 3:17).

Interestingly, the words "defile" and "destroy" are the exact same word in Greek — the word *phtheiro*, which means *to spoil, plunder, destroy, empty*, or *wipe out*. How you treat the Church is exactly how God is going to treat you. If you bless the Church, God will bless you. But if you spoil, plunder, or destroy the Church — if you empty the Church of its truth or power — the Lord will allow the same actions to come upon you.

It is actually the law of sowing and reaping that kicks into action (*see* Galatians 6:7,8). Anyone who handles the house of God — the people of God — improperly, the law of sowing and reaping will bring the same treatment into his or her own life.

This may not be popular in today's spiritual climate, but this is the teaching of Scripture. The absence of this teaching has resulted in an absence of the fear of God in the Church today. When this is taught and understood, seriousness and sobriety will come to God's people. Yes, He wants to bless us. Jesus came to give us life and life more abundantly (*see* John 10:10). But we also need to realize that if we mishandle the Church and refuse to repent, we are going to reap the same kind of treatment in our own lives. This is exactly what the woman Jezebel in the church of Thyatira was facing.

STUDY QUESTIONS

Study to shew thyself approved unto God, a workman that needeth not to be ashamed, rightly dividing the word of truth.
— 2 Timothy 2:15

The Church is the Body of Christ. It is His Bride. It is made up of people from every tribe, every nation, and every continent around the world. How we treat God's people (His Church) is very important to Him, as we have seen in the case of Jezebel and her mistreatment of the believers in the church of Thyatira.

1. In Matthew 18:5-9, what does Jesus say about your treatment of "little ones" in the Church? (Also consider Matthew 10:42 and Mark 9:42-47.)
2. Carefully read Jesus' words in Luke 12:42-48. Identify the characteristics of a *wise* and *faithful servant* that we are to emulate and the qualities of a *wicked servant* we are to avoid.

PRACTICAL APPLICATION

> But be ye doers of the word, and not hearers only,
> deceiving your own selves.
> —James 1:22

The woman Jezebel at the church in Thyatira heard the voice of the Lord pleading with her to repent, but she willfully continued doing what she knew was wrong. Jesus had no other choice but to deal with her and put a stop to her destructive doctrines.

1. How does this lesson put a holy reverential fear of God in you regarding the way you treat fellow believers? (Consider Romans 14:10-13; 2 Corinthians 5:9,10.)
2. Have you mishandled a brother or sister in the Body of Christ? Is there someone you need to go to and humbly apologize for misleading or mistreating them? Take time now to ask the Holy Spirit to thoroughly search your heart and show you anything that displeases Him (*see* Psalm 139:23,24). Repent of any sin, and carry out any action steps He prompts you to take.

TOPIC

The Depths of Satan Inside the Church

SCRIPTURES

1. **Revelation 2:18-24** — And unto the angel of the church in Thyatira write; These things saith the Son of God, who hath his eyes like unto a flame of fire, and his feet are like fine brass. I know thy works, and charity, and service, and faith, and thy patience, and thy works; and the last to be more than the first. Notwithstanding I have a few things against thee, because thou sufferest that woman Jezebel, which calleth herself a prophetess, to teach and to seduce my servants to commit fornication, and to eat things sacrificed unto idols. And I gave her space to repent of her fornication; and she repented not. Behold, I will cast her into a bed, and them that commit adultery with her into great tribulation, except they repent of their deeds. And I will kill her children with death; and all the churches shall know that I am he which searcheth the reins and hearts: and I will give unto every one of you according to your works. But unto you I say, and unto the rest in Thyatira, as many as have not this doctrine, and which have not known the depths of Satan, as they speak; I will put upon you none other burden.

GREEK WORDS

1. "I say" — **λέγω** (*lego*): direct speech; I say
2. "doctrine" — **τὴν διδαχὴν** (*ten didachen*): with a definite article, well-packaged information
3. "depths" — **βαθύς** (*bathus*): depths; alleged deep places; used to depict depths of the sea
4. "Satan" — **Σατανᾶς** (*satanas*): an adversary who hates and conspires against
5. "burden" — **βάρος** (*baros*): a heavy or crushing weight

SYNOPSIS

When the preachers of the Gospel arrived in the ancient city of Thyatira, they came face to face with a very dark and disturbing place. It was a pagan city filled with politicians, military officers, and thousands of rough Roman soldiers. Yet with the anointing of the Holy Spirit, these ministers of truth boldly proclaimed the Good News of Jesus Christ, and a thriving church was born.

Of course, no church is without problems, and Thyatira was no exception. In fact, it had some serious issues. The pastor and certain people were permitting a woman in leadership to teach false doctrine that was leading people astray. Those involved with this error were to repent and realign themselves with the pure teaching of Scripture, but they had not heeded Jesus' command. As a result, *the depths of Satan* had been let loose inside the church.

The emphasis of this lesson:

As a result of Jezebel's teaching and the people who supported it, the depths of Satan had been unleashed in the church of Thyatira. But to all those who rejected her doctrine of compromise, Jesus was pleased.

Jesus Was Fully Aware of the Situation in the Church of Thyatira

Jesus spoke a strong message to the church of Thyatira in Revelation 2. In verses 18 and 19, He said, "And unto the angel of the church in Thyatira write; These things saith the Son of God, who hath his eyes like unto a flame of fire, and his feet are like fine brass. I know thy works, and charity, and service, and faith, and thy patience, and thy works; and the last to be more than the first."

We have determined that the "angel" of the church of Thyatira to whom Jesus was speaking was *the pastor*. A pastor's primary, God-given responsibility is to be God's voice to the church. He is to receive the messages God is speaking to the church, incorporate them into his own life, and feed them to the congregation he shepherds in the power of the Holy Spirit.

To each of the seven churches Christ spoke to in Revelation 2 and 3, He said, "I know thy works." The phrase "I know" is the Greek word *oida*, which means, *"I know; I've seen; I've personally observed with My own eyes your works. What I know about you is not what has been reported to Me by an angel or anyone else. I have personally witnessed it Myself."*

This brings us to the word "works," which we have seen is the Greek word *erga*, and it means *every activity, deed, and action.* The use of this word is the same as Jesus saying, "I know absolutely everything there is to know about you; there is nothing about you I do not know." This was a great church that was making a great impact in the lives of the people in the region.

The Strike Against the Church Deeply Disturbed Him

There was, however, something going on in the church that was deeply disturbing to Jesus and that He had to address. In Revelation 2:20, He said, "Notwithstanding I have a few things against thee...."

We have seen that the word "notwithstanding" is the Greek word *alla*, and it marks *a pause* or *a break* in the text. Jesus was transitioning from His words of commendation to His words of correction. Essentially, He was saying, "In spite of all these good qualities I've just noted, there's an issue I have against you."

The phrase "I have" is from the Greek word *echo*, and it means *I hold* or *I embrace.* It carries the idea of holding something very close and personal to one's heart. Jesus had an issue He held very deeply "against" the church of Thyatira. The word "against" is the Greek word *kata*, which describes *a downward mark or strike.* Despite all the marvelous works being done in the church, Jesus said, "I personally hold a serious strike against you."

He continued saying, "...Because thou sufferest that woman Jezebel, which calleth herself a prophetess, to teach and to seduce my servants to commit fornication, and to eat things sacrificed unto idols" (Revelation 2:20). Again, notice the word "prophetess" — the Greek word *prophetes.* It describes *one who speaks on behalf of God.*

Jezebel was claiming to be God's voice to the people, but she was speaking a doctrine of compromise that was out of sync with Scripture. Her basic message was this: "Relax and don't be so strict. Lower your standards and be more inclusive of the people in the world. This will help you blend in and be accepted by others." Her seducing words were leading a number of believers in Thyatira to commit fornication, which deeply disturbed Jesus.

The truth is, if Jezebel was truly a "prophetess" who spoke on behalf of God, she would have been saying what God says. Regardless of whether or not it was comfortable or enjoyable to speak, she would have echoed the truth, not modified it to suit her own interests. Society and culture are constantly in a state of change, but *truth never changes*. As God's prophetic voice to the Church and the world, we are to speak only what He is saying — no more, no less.

He Gave Jezebel Time To Repent, But She Refused

Jesus said, "I gave her space to repent of her fornication; and she repented not" (Revelation 2:21). The word "fornication" is the Greek word *pornea*, which describes *any sexual activity outside of marriage*. By using this word, Jesus was saying, "I've given Jezebel a specific amount of time to repent of her *spiritual adultery*." By encouraging people to compromise God's standards of holiness, the woman Jesus called Jezebel was inciting them to commit spiritual adultery.

As believers, we are the temple of God and His Spirit lives in us (*see* 1 Corinthians 3:16). First Corinthians 3:17 says, "If any man defile the temple of God, him shall God destroy; for the temple of God is holy, which temple ye are." Jezebel was defiling God's temple, and Jesus warned her to stop it. He personally gave her "space" — the Greek word *chronos*, meaning *a specified season of time* — to repent. But Scripture says she "willed not to repent of her fornication."

To deal with Jezebel, Jesus said, "Behold, I will cast her into a bed, and them that commit adultery with her into great tribulation, except they repent of their deeds" (Revelation 2:22). The word "except" here indicates that Jesus was hopeful that Jezebel might repent and realign herself with the truth. He never wants to deal harshly with or bring judgment on His people. But if they will not repent and if they deliberately choose to keep doing wrong, He is left with no other choice.

In verse 23, Jesus declared, "And I will kill her children with death; and all the churches shall know that I am he which searcheth the reins and hearts: and I will give unto every one of you according to your works."

Not Everyone Supported Jezebel's Efforts

In Revelation 2:24, Jesus spoke to the believers of Thyatira — those who had *not* supported Jezebel's false doctrine. To them, He declared, "But unto you I say, and unto the rest in Thyatira, as many as have not this doctrine, and which have *not* known the depths of Satan, as they speak; I will put upon you none other burden."

The words "I say" is the Greek word *lego*, and it is *very direct speech*. By including this word, it was the equivalent of Jesus saying, "Listen to Me; I'm speaking to you, and not just you but unto the rest." The phrase "unto the rest" in the Greek means *"unto the balance of you — unto all of you, as many as have not this false doctrine."*

The Greek translation of the word "doctrine" is *ten didachen*. It includes a definite article and describes *well-packaged information.* This tells us that the deadly doctrine of compromise Jezebel had introduced into the church of Thyatira was not blatant error; it was carefully and cleverly disguised. It would be like taking a small amount of poison and mixing it together with a larger amount of quality food. Jezebel was successful in getting people to swallow her deception because it was unrecognizable in its alluring package.

The Holy Spirit has much to say in the New Testament about the proliferation of seducing doctrine in the last days. First Timothy 4:1 says, "Now the Spirit speaketh expressly, that in the latter times some shall depart from the faith, giving heed to seducing spirits, and doctrines of devils." In this passage, the Holy Spirit forecasts that at the very end of the age, when there is no more time remaining in this present season, a breeding ground for error will fester not only in the secular world, but also within the Church.

For anyone with a discerning eye, it is unmistakably clear that these seductive spirits are already at work. One observing the absurd moral developments in various sectors of society can turn his focus on certain quarters of the Body of Christ and recognize the camouflaged error that is also trying to emerge in the Church in our times.

In the Christian world today, there are some spiritual leaders who seek a dangerous truce with the world under the guise of inclusiveness and compromise. (This was what the woman called Jezebel in Thyatira was doing.) Many of these leaders once held strong doctrinal positions. However, over time they began to shape their beliefs to meld with the changing moral climate of society — and in the process, they produced a Gospel message very different from the one presented in the Bible.

The problem of worldly compromise continues to spread in the Church, and even some visible Christian leaders are promoting this trend. It is therefore vital for mature believers to be able to recognize the process of seduction that seeks to "repackage" the Gospel — adapting and diluting it in an attempt to make it more palatable.

'The Depths of Satan'

Keep in mind, the Jezebel in Thyatira was calling herself a "prophetess" — claiming to be the voice of God. It seems she alleged to have a "new revelation" from God, but it was really nothing more than a modification of the truth. What she was saying was not really from the mouth of God. It was a highly sophisticated repackaging of the truth, and Jesus called it "the depths of Satan" (*see* Revelation 2:24).

The word "depths" is the Greek word *bathus*, and it was used to depict *the depths of the sea*. It describes *depths* or *alleged deep places*. It's very likely that Jezebel said, "I'm on the cutting edge of new, progressive thinking. I can see what we as the Church need to do. Being more inclusive and melding with society is the direction for our future." With great care, she repackaged the truth so the believers in Thyatira could blend in with society and no longer be viewed as narrow-minded, bigoted, or relics of the past. In this woman's mind, the acceptance of Christians by society was of utmost importance. This would ensure they could keep their jobs, maintain a steady income, and not pay a price for their faith.

The problem with Jezebel's doctrine was that it didn't line up with the truth. Jesus said, "If the world hate you, ye know that it hated me before it hated you. If ye were of the world, the world would love his own: but because ye are not of the world, but I have chosen you out of the world, therefore the world hateth you" (John 15:18,19). If you're experiencing a little persecution from time to time, it's probably an indicator that you're doing something right.

As believers, we are the Church. In Greek, the word "church" is *ekklesia*, which is a compound of the word *ek*, meaning *out*, and a form of the word *kaleo*, meaning *to be called or summoned*. We are God's *called-out ones* who are to be separate and live differently. He said, "…Be ye holy; for I am holy" (1 Peter 1:16). The Greek word for "holy" is *hagios*, which means *separate, consecrated, different from everyone else*. Any teaching that claims you don't have to be different from the rest of the world is false doctrine.

Jesus' Promise to the Faithful

Jesus called Jezebel's repackaging of the truth "the depths of Satan" (*see* Revelation 2:24). The word "Satan" is the Greek word *Satanas*, and it describes *an adversary who hates and conspires against another*. Basically, Jesus was saying, "This false doctrine is a demonic conspiracy devised by Satan and voiced through someone influential in the church of Thyatira to take it down."

Jesus continued with this promise: "…As many as have not known this doctrine, and which have not known the depths of Satan, as they speak; I will put upon you none other burden" (Revelation 2:24). The word "known" here is from the Greek word *ginosko*, and in the context of this particular verse, it means *as many of you as have not embraced, participated in, or intimately known by personal experience this doctrine; you've refrained from it — you and all those with you.* Jesus said, "…I will put upon you none other burden."

The word "burden" in Greek is *baros*, and it describes *a heavy or crushing weight*. To all the people who did not swallow, support, or spread Jezebel's doctrine of compromise or add to "the depths of Satan" in the church, Jesus was pleased and had nothing against them. They had chosen *not* to cooperate with the devil by supporting or teaching compromise. They had made a decision to stick with Scripture, live right, and walk separately from the world.

Friend, when you stick with the truth, it will sometimes put you in a difficult position — but in the long run, *you win*. Jesus is proud of your stance for Him, and He is cheering you on. He is calling you, just as He called the believers in Thyatira, to stay with Scripture, live a separate life, and refuse to modify the faith, even if everybody else seems to be losing his or her mind.

In our final lesson, you will see what it means to hold fast, overcome, and occupy until He comes. There are rich rewards waiting for those who do!

STUDY QUESTIONS

Study to shew thyself approved unto God, a workman that needeth
not to be ashamed, rightly dividing the word of truth.
— 2 Timothy 2:15

God's Word says, "The thing that hath been, it is that which shall be...
there is no new thing under the sun" (Ecclesiastes 1:9). History does
indeed repeat itself. Consider how the history of Thyatira is being repeated
in our own time.

1. What similarities can you identify between what is happening in parts
    of the modern Church today and what was taking place in the church
    of Thyatira?
2. What responsibility has Jesus given to His pastors to carry out when
    they are made aware that someone is teaching wrong doctrine to the
    people under their charge?
3. How does God deal with unfaithful shepherds who teach false doc-
    trine to His flock (*see* Revelation 2:22,23)?

PRACTICAL APPLICATION

But be ye doers of the word, and not hearers only,
deceiving your own selves.
— James 1:22

1. The doctrine of error taught by Jezebel and embraced by certain
    members in Thyatira is a sobering reminder of the importance of
    sticking with Scripture. How about you? Do you truly know what the
    Bible teaches? If you were to stand before Jesus Christ today, would
    He say that you are a person who is committed to the pure teaching
    of Scripture or one given to a doctrine of compromise?
2. Jesus said, "Behold, I am sending you out like sheep in the midst
    of wolves; be wary and wise as serpents, and be innocent (harmless,
    guileless, and without falsity) as doves" (Matthew 10:16 *AMPC*). How
    might this principle look in your day-to-day existence? Pray and ask
    the Lord to make this truth a reality in your life.

TOPIC

Hold Fast and Occupy
Until Jesus Comes

SCRIPTURES

1. **Revelation 2:18-29** — And unto the angel of the church in Thyatira write; These things saith the Son of God, who hath his eyes like unto a flame of fire, and his feet are like fine brass. I know thy works, and charity, and service, and faith, and thy patience, and thy works; and the last to be more than the first. Notwithstanding I have a few things against thee, because thou sufferest that woman Jezebel, which calleth herself a prophetess, to teach and to seduce my servants to commit fornication, and to eat things sacrificed unto idols. And I gave her space to repent of her fornication; and she repented not. Behold, I will cast her into a bed, and them that commit adultery with her into great tribulation, except they repent of their deeds. And I will kill her children with death; and all the churches shall know that I am he which searcheth the reins and hearts: and I will give unto every one of you according to your works. But unto you I say, and unto the rest in Thyatira, as many as have not this doctrine, and which have not known the depths of Satan, as they speak; I will put upon you none other burden. But that which ye have already hold fast till I come. And he that overcometh, and keepeth my works unto the end, to him will I give power over the nations. And he shall rule them with a rod of iron; as the vessels of a potter shall they be broken to shivers: even as I received of my Father. And I will give him the morning star. He that hath an ear, let him hear what the Spirit saith unto the churches.

2. **Romans 8:37** — Nay, in all these things we are more than conquerors through him that loved us.

GREEK WORDS

1. "ye have" — ἔχετε (*echete*): have; hold; embrace

2. "hold fast" — **κρατέω** (*krateo*): to seize; to take hold of; to firmly grip; to apprehend; denotes strength, power, victory over something; pictures taking something by force

3. "till" — **ἄχρι** (*achri*): until, to the time that

4. "I come" — **ἥκω** (*heko*): I have come; I have arrived

5. "overcometh" — **νικάω** (*nikao*): tense means one who is overcoming; a victor; a champion; one who conquers, defeats, masters, overcomes, overwhelms, or is victorious; used to portray athletes who mastered their sport and reigned as champions; describes a military victory against an enemy

6. "keepeth" — **τηρέω** (*tereo*): a watch of soldiers to protect; soldiers who were faithful and committed to their charge, regardless of assaults or attackers encountered; depicts a need to stand on guard over what has been entrusted to a person; careful and watchful attitude in any situation

7. "works" — **ἔργα** (*erga*): deeds, actions, or activities

8. "unto" — **ἄχρι** (*achri*): until; up to the time

9. "end" — **τέλος** (*telos*): completion; a climax; ultimate conclusion

10. "will I give" — **δώσω** (*doso*): the future personal form of **δίδωμι**; I will personally give

11. "power" — **ἐξουσία** (*exousia*): delegated authority or influence

12. "shall rule" — **ποιμαίνω** (*poinaino*): to shepherd; occurs 11 times in the New Testament, always in reference to the task of shepherding

13. "rod" — **ῥάβδος** (*hrabdos*): a shepherd's staff; a staff of authority

14. "iron" — **σιδήρεος** (*sidereos*): something made of iron

15. "I will give" — **δώσω** (*doso*): the future personal form of **δίδωμι**; I will personally give

16. "morning star" — **ἀστέρα τὸν πρωϊνόν** (*astera ton proinon*): the early morning star; refers to Jesus' perfect brightness; the brilliance of the morning sun as it breaks through the darkness of night

SYNOPSIS

The city of Pergamum was an extremely powerful and wealthy city that eastern invaders longed to attack and plunder of all its goods. To combat and put a stop to this threat, the leaders of Pergamum built a barricade, and that barricade was called the city of Thyatira — a weaponized military outpost staffed with thousands of soldiers ready to defend and defeat any intruders.

A church was established in Thyatira in the First Century, and because the city was a military outpost with thousands of soldiers, we can be sure that many of the military personnel were coming to Christ. In fact, a large number of these soldiers would have been members of this church that was thriving and making a difference. Yet as amazing as this church was, it was not without problems.

With great love and care, Jesus addressed every issue, giving the people ample time to repent and make things right. He called the believers there to be overcomers. As a congregation in part comprised of military personnel, the church of Thyatira knew all about overcoming. It is a mindset that expects to experience one victory after another victory — the same conviction Jesus wants to develop in us today. And to the Christians who consistently overcome — both then and now — Jesus promised great blessing.

The emphasis of this lesson:

God's plan for your life is *victory* — from the time we're saved until we see Jesus face to face. Like the believers in Thyatira, we are to hold fast and occupy until He comes.

You Are Called To Be God's Voice

Once more, let us review the message of Jesus Christ to the church of Thyatira in the second chapter of Revelation. He said, "And unto the angel of the church in Thyatira write; These things saith the Son of God, who hath his eyes like unto a flame of fire, and his feet are like fine brass. I know thy works, and charity, and service, and faith, and thy patience, and thy works; and the last to be more than the first. Notwithstanding I have a few things against thee, because thou sufferest that woman Jezebel, which calleth herself a prophetess, to teach and to seduce my servants to commit fornication, and to eat things sacrificed unto idols" (Revelation 2:18-20).

Interestingly, the phrase "which calleth" in Greek would better be translated, "who alleges that she is." Jezebel professed to be a prophetess who spoke on behalf of God. She claimed to be super-spiritual and to have discernment and insight that no one else had. She declared to be on the cutting edge of a new doctrine from Heaven — but she wasn't speaking the Word of God. What she was teaching was well-packaged false doctrine that was seducing believers to return to sinful ways.

Seize the Opportunity To Self-Correct

Jezebel, the self-proclaimed prophetess, was permitted to teach, even though her false teaching was seducing Gods' servants to commit fornication and eat things sacrificed unto idols. Jesus said, "I gave her space to repent of her fornication; and she repented not" (Revelation 2:21). We have learned that the earliest New Testament manuscripts show this verse to read, "She willed not to repent out of her fornication." In other words, Jezebel knew God was instructing her to stop teaching the error she was teaching and to turn back to the truth of Scripture, but she refused to cooperate.

God gives all of us an opportunity to repent of wrong attitudes, beliefs, and actions, just as He did for Jezebel of Thyatira. But the choice to do so is ours. Jezebel passed up the season of time (the "space") that Jesus graciously gave her to repent of her sin and correct her ways. If you know He is giving you "space" to repent of something you've done, seize the opportunity! The time to self-correct is a precious opportunity, not to be wasted.

The Bible reveals that once the season to repent and make things right expires, Jesus is left with no other choice than to respond with correction. For Jezebel's failure to repent, Jesus said, "Behold, I will cast her into a bed, and them that commit adultery with her into great tribulation…" (Revelation 2:22).

We have seen that the word "bed" in Greek can be translated as *a bed* or *a couch* and is often used to describe *a sickbed*. It is also the same word for *a funeral bier*. By using this word, Jesus was saying, "I am about to put this woman out of commission. I'm going to put an end to her, her deeds, and her doctrines. And all those that commit adultery with her are going to experience a period of great crushing pressure."

In Jesus' mercy, He added, "…except they repent of their deeds" (Revelation 2:22). The word "except" indicates that Jesus is still hopeful that Jezebel and her co-conspirators will repent — even if it is at the very last moment. If they do, the pending judgment He warned them of will be averted.

Christ offers us the same grace and mercy to turn away from sin and toward Him.

Jesus Is Pleased With and Proud of Those Who Refuse To Compromise

To those in Thyatira who refused to repent, Jesus said, "And I will kill her children with death…" (Revelation 2:23). The word "children" is the Greek word *tekna*, which means *children* or *offspring*. The implication here is that Jesus will kill what Jezebel has produced with her seducing doctrine, and He will kill it with "death." The word "death" in Greek is *thanatos*, which signifies *finality*. Essentially, Jesus was saying, "I'm going to bring a decisive end to the rotten fruit this woman and her false doctrine have given birth to."

What will result from Jesus' actions? He declared, "…All the churches shall know that I am he which searcheth the reins and hearts: and I will give unto every one of you according to your works." He then offered a word of encouragement to all those who had kept themselves from compromise. "But unto you I say, and unto the rest in Thyatira, as many as have not this doctrine, and which have not known the depths of Satan, as they speak; I will put upon you none other burden" (Revelation 2:24).

In our last lesson, we discovered the meaning of the phrase "the depths of Satan." The word "depths" is the Greek word *bathus*, and it signifies *something very deep*. Jezebel and her accomplices claimed to be moving into new depths of spiritual insight — that they were on the cutting edge of new progressive thinking. But that was not the case. The "depths" of spirituality they were moving into was the "depths of Satan."

The word "Satan" is the Greek word *satanas*, and it describes *an adversary who hates and conspires against someone*. Hence, by using the phrase "the depths of Satan," Jesus was saying, "Satan himself has hatched this conspiracy in the church in an attempt to take it down, and he has done it through the well-packaged, damnable doctrine of compromise." On the other hand, Jesus was pleased with those who chose not to swallow, support, or spread Jezebel's false doctrine, promising not to put any other burden on them.

Hold Fast to What You Have

Christ continued His words to the faithful believers in Thyatira, stating, "But that which ye have already hold fast till I come" (Revelation 2:25). Ironically, in the original Greek, the word "already" seen in the *King James Version* doesn't exist. It simply says, "But that which ye have hold fast till I come."

The phrase "ye have" is the Greek word *echete*, which means *to have, to hold*, or *to embrace*. Thus, the phrase, "that which ye have already," could be translated, "That which you have already obtained; that which you already hold; that which you have already achieved; the territory you have already gained." To *that*, Jesus said we are to "hold fast till I come."

The words "hold fast" is a translation from the well-known Greek word *krateo*, which means *to seize; to take hold of; to firmly grip*; or *to apprehend*. It denotes *strength, power, and victory over something*. It pictures *taking something by force*. By Jesus' use of the word *krateo*, He was saying, "That which you have already embraced, the territory you have already gained, the victory you have already apprehended — wrap your arms around it. Use all your strength to grasp it, and refuse to let anyone take it from you till I come."

The word "till" in Greek is *achri*, which means *until* or *to the time that*. The phrase "I come" is a translation of the Greek word *heko*, which means *I have come* or *I have arrived*. We are to faithfully hold fast to all that we have — our faith, God's promises, the territory we've gained — until the very moment Jesus visibly appears on the scene.

When you feel yourself becoming weary, press into the presence of God and hold fast to Him. In those moments, your faith is being tested, and the trying of your faith "worketh patience," which is *endurance* (*see* James 1:3). The word "worketh" describes a type of chemical reaction from the top of your head to the bottom of your feet. When you hold fast to your faith in God during times of testing, an amazing thing takes place. His Spirit literally fills you with supernatural *endurance* — the Greek word *hupomeno*, which describes *the ability to endure; supernatural stamina; durability*, or *to hang on and never give up*.

If you are weary, refuse to give up and then *hold fast*. As you do, God's Spirit will join Himself to you and give you the divine durability and stamina you need to succeed.

You Are *More Than a Conqueror*

In Revelation 2:26, Jesus said, "And he that overcometh, and keepeth my works unto the end, to him will I give power over the nations." The word "overcometh" in this verse is the Greek word *nikao*, and the tense indicates *one who is overcoming*. It describes *a victor, a champion*; or *one who conquers, defeats, masters, overcomes, overwhelms, or is victorious*. This word has been used to portray athletes who mastered their sport and reigned as champions. It can also describe a military victory against an enemy. By using the word *nikao* — translated here as *overcometh* — Jesus has made it clear that He has called us to be overcomers from now to the end of our lives.

The apostle Paul confirmed this in Romans 8:37, declaring, "Nay, in all these things we are more than conquerors through him that loved us." He said we are called to be "more than conquerors," which is a phrase translated from the Greek word *hupernikos*. This word is a compound of the words *huper* and *nikos* — and it appears that this was the very first time the compound word *hupernikos* was used in Greek literature. Paul literally had to create a word to describe the level of victory we are given in Christ Jesus!

The word *huper* signifies *over, above, and beyond*. It describes something *great, higher, better, more than a match for, utmost, paramount*, or *foremost*. It depicts something that is *far beyond measure* and conveys the idea of *superiority*. This word *huper* means to be *first-rate, first-class, top-notch, unsurpassed, unequaled*, and *unrivaled by any person or anything*. We derive the word *super* from the word *huper*.

Under the direction of the Holy Spirit, Paul chose the word *huper* to denote what kind of conquerors we are to be in Christ. We are *huper-conquerors*. In other words, we are *superior conquerors who are more than a match for any adversary*. We are *utmost and paramount conquerors who are first-class, top-notch, unsurpassed, unequaled, and unrivaled*. All this meaning is packed into just the first word Paul selected.

The second word is *nikos* — translated here as "conquerors" — and it describes an *overcomer, conqueror, champion, victor*, or *master*. It is a dramatic picture of *an overwhelming prevailing force that is altogether victorious*. By calling us "more than conquerors," Paul is saying that in Christ, we are *overwhelming conquerors, paramount champions*, and *enormous overcomers*.

This phrase is so bursting with power that one could translate it, "We are a phenomenal, walloping, conquering force!"

So when Jesus calls us "overcomers" and "more than conquerors," He isn't describing a single victory followed by a string of losses. He is declaring that in Him we are victory-producing machines — experiencing one triumph after another triumph from now until the time He comes.

The Faithful Will Be Rewarded With Rulership

Looking again at Revelation 2:26, Jesus said, "And he that overcometh, and keepeth my works unto the end, to him will I give power over the nations." Notice the word "keepeth." It is translated from the Greek word *tereo*, and it describes *soldiers who were faithful and committed to their charge, regardless of assaults or attackers encountered.* It depicts *a need to stand guard over what has been entrusted to a person* or a *careful and watchful attitude in any situation.*

Jesus said we are to keep His "works unto the end." The word "works" is the Greek word *erga*, which describes *deeds, actions, or activities.* The word "unto" is again the Greek word *achri*, and it means *until* or *to the time.* Furthermore, the word "end" in Greek is *telos*, which describes *completion, a climax, or the ultimate conclusion.* It indicates *the end of the age when Jesus returns.* The conclusion or completion of our walk of faith will not be concluded or come to its full, maximized maturity until we have done all that we have been called to do and we see Jesus face to face.

If we will faithfully stand guard over the deeds and activities that have been entrusted to us until the time Jesus returns, He said that He "will give" us "power over the nations." In Greek, the words "I will give" are very personal. It is the equivalent of Jesus saying, "I will *personally* give you power over the nations." The word "power" is the Greek word *exousia*, and it describes *delegated authority or influence.*

When Jesus finds you faithfully standing and refusing to surrender the territory He has assigned to you, He will promote you into a new realm of spiritual authority. And with your new level of authority, you "...shall rule them with a rod of iron..." (Revelation 2:27).

In Greek, the phrase "shall rule" is the word *poinaino*, which means *to shepherd.* It occurs 11 times in the New Testament and is always used in reference to the task of shepherding. As a faithful conqueror, you will shepherd the nations with a "rod of iron." The word "rod" is the Greek word *hrabdos*, and it describes *a shepherd's staff*. It is *a staff of authority forged out of iron*.

In Psalm 23:4, David said of the Lord, "…Thy rod and thy staff they comfort me." A shepherd used his rod to direct his sheep and pull them back into line. If necessary, he also used it to discipline the sheep. Therefore, when David said, "…Thy rod and thy staff they comfort me," he was saying, "It is a comfort to me, Lord, to know You are going to use Your rod to direct me in the way I need to go, pull me back in line, and correct me if I need to be disciplined."

This understanding lets us know that when Jesus said we shall rule the nations with a "rod of iron," He was saying, "I want to give you delegated authority to shepherd other people. With a rod of iron, you will be able to direct them in the right way, pull them back in line, and bring loving correction if needed."

'Lord, Give Us Ears To Hear What You Are Saying'

This brings us to Revelation 2:28, where Jesus said, "And I will give him the morning star." Again, we see this phrase "I will give" — the Greek word *doso*, which means, *"I will personally give."* What will Jesus personally give? He said, "the morning star," which in Greek means *the early morning star*. It refers to *Jesus' perfect brightness* or *the brilliance of the morning sun as it breaks through the darkness of night*.

If you will hold fast and occupy until Jesus comes, He will make sure you see the light of day. The darkness that you have been dealing with will no longer dominate you. It doesn't stand a chance when the light of the morning star begins to break forth in your life!

Jesus concluded His message to the pastor and the people of the church of Thyatira saying, "He that hath an ear, let him hear what the Spirit saith unto the churches" (Revelation 2:29). The fact that Jesus said, "He that hath an ear," lets us know that not everyone has an ear to hear what Jesus is saying. That is why we need to pray, "Lord, give us ears to hear what You are saying to the churches."

Notice the word "churches" is plural. This tells us that every message to all seven churches in Revelation 2 and 3 applies to every believer everywhere and in every age who has an ear to hear.

Friend, Jesus is coming! It is *not* time to let go and give up. It is time to press into God's presence and hold fast and occupy until He comes. It's time to hold on, dig in, and make a decision that *you're not budging.* You are going to maintain the territory God has assigned to you all the way until you see Him face to face. You can do it with the power of the Holy Spirit!

STUDY QUESTIONS

Study to shew thyself approved unto God, a workman that needeth not to be ashamed, rightly dividing the word of truth.
— 2 Timothy 2:15

1. God's Word spoken from your mouth is the one weapon that can truly transform society. According to Romans 1:16, why should you not be ashamed of the Gospel? What do Hebrews 4:12 and James 1:21 declare will happen as you ready, study, and speak the Word?

2. All of us become weary at times in our walk of faith. But God has promised to infuse us with His divine strength as we sincerely seek His presence. Carefully read His promises to you in Isaiah 40:28-31 and Philippians 4:13. Commit these truths to memory, and use them to write a brief prayer to receive God's empowerment.

PRACTICAL APPLICATION

But be ye doers of the word, and not hearers only, deceiving your own selves.
— James 1:22

1. Jesus instructs us to "hold fast" till He comes (*see* Revelation 2:25). Is there anything you have obtained and achieved in your walk of faith that seems to be slipping away? If so, what is it? What practical and spiritual steps can you take to tighten your grip on these things?

2. Take a few moments to read and reflect on the meaning of the phrase "more than conquerors." Then in your own words, write a personal declaration stating that *you* are *more than a conqueror in Christ Jesus.*

3. To experience an even greater impact from your declaration of truth, take the next two weeks to speak it out loud *over yourself* as well as *over your spouse and children.* Journal the positive effects that you witness as a result of speaking this truth.

A Prayer To Receive Salvation

If you've never received Jesus as your Savior and Lord, now is the time for you to experience the new life Jesus wants to give you! To receive God's gift of salvation that can be obtained through Jesus alone, pray this prayer from your heart:

Jesus, I repent of my sin and receive You as my Savior and Lord. Wash away my sin with Your precious blood and make me completely new. I thank You that my sin is removed, and Satan no longer has any right to lay claim on me. Through Your empowering grace, I faithfully promise that I will serve You as my Lord for the rest of my life.

If you just prayed this prayer of salvation, you are born again! You are a brand-new creation in Christ! Would you please let us know of your decision by going to **renner.org/salvation**? We would love to connect with you and pray for you as you begin your new life in Christ.

Scriptures for further study: John 3:16; John 14:6; Acts 4:12; Ephesians 1:7; Hebrews 10:19,20; 1 Peter 1:18,19; Romans 10:9,10; Colossians 1:13; 2 Corinthians 5:17; Romans 6:4; 1 Peter 1:3

www.ingramcontent.com/pod-product-compliance
Lightning Source LLC
Chambersburg PA
CBHW071625040426
42452CB00009B/1499